Church-State Relations:
An Annotated Bibliography

Garland Reference Library of Social Science (Vol. 24)

Also by Albert J. Menendez

The Bitter Harvest: Church and State in Northern Ireland
The Sherlock Holmes Quizbook
The Best of Church and State (editor)
The American Political Quizbook

Church-State Relations:
An Annotated Bibliography

Albert J. Menendez

Garland Publishing, Inc., New York & London

1976

Library of Congress Cataloging in Publication Data

Menendez, Albert J
  Church-state relations.

  (Garland reference library of social science ; v. 24)
  Includes index.
  1. Church and state--Bibliography. I. Title.
Z7776.72.M45 1976 [BV630.2] 016.2617 75-24894
ISBN 0-8240-9956-7

To Shirley, My Wife

Contents

CONTENTS

Introduction

The perceptive British historian Lord Bryce once observed that "Half the wars of Europe, half the internal troubles that have vexed European States... have arisen from theological differences or from the rival claims of church and state." Because of the central importance of church-state relations in Western history, it is necessary for informed individuals to have some knowledge of this crucial field.

This annotated bibliography seeks to fill the existing void in this complex, amorphous field. Knowledge of church-state problems and religious liberty concerns is often secured by accident or in incidental ways. I hope to make a more systematic methodology available to students and scholars by the preparation of this work.

We shall begin with a consideration of the historical development, giving primary emphasis to the United States and Great Britain. All of the works annotated will be in English and most have been published since 1875. Closely related to the historical overview will be a listing of books dealing with the struggle to achieve the free exercise of religious expression.

Necessarily related to the general topic are books dealing with religious conflict, primarily between Catholics and Protestants, which significantly affected the role of the state in religion. Primary and secondary sources will be included. Considerations of religious influences on governmental decisions, political actions, public policies, and elections will be annotated.

Education has loomed as a central battlefield within which important church-state decisions were made. Books dealing with parochial schools, public funding of religiously-affiliated educational institutions, and the vast, complex problem of religion in the public school context will be included.

INTRODUCTION

Interfaith relations have played a considerable role in the formulation of policies relating to religious toleration by civil authorities. The way in which one religion regarded another often determined whether the society and its civil laws reflected repressive or pluralistic impulses. Hence, a listing of the exhaustive literature of religious controversy is in order.

Finally, a consideration of the role played by the Vatican in church-state relations world-wide is a necessity. A considerable body of literature, indeed almost constituting a science of Vaticanology, has been published in the last century. Both sympathetic and critical appraisals will be incorporated in the work.

This bibliography includes only English language, full-length books which treat a subject in some depth or completeness. I have not included pamphlets, booklets, or periodical articles because they are generally inadequate. Doctoral dissertations have not been included. Scholars wishing to consult them should check the *Journal of Church and State,* which lists germane dissertations in each issue. It should be reiterated that this is a selective rather than exhaustive compilation.

Albert J. Menendez
Silver Spring, Maryland
September 1975

Chapter I

GENERAL BIBLIOGRAPHIES

Works dealing with church-state relations and religious liberty questions are included in a number of general bibliographies. We are not including periodical references, dissertation abstracts, or archival sources.

Barber, Cyril J. The Minister's Library. Baker Book House, Grand Rapids, 1974.
A selective but comprehensive evaluation of several thousand volumes available to serious Protestant clergy. Contains many significant church-state related items.

Bernard, Jack F. and John J. Delaney. A Guide to Catholic Reading. Doubleday Image Books, New York, 1966.
A highly selective look at 750 important books for Catholic readers. Includes a full chapter on "Church and State" and "The Papacy". Thoughtfully annotated, the volume includes succinct introductory essays to each section.

Brown, Stephen J. An Introduction to Catholic Booklore. Burns and Oates, London, 1933.
A classic introduction to Catholic bibliographic sources.

Brown, Stephen J. and Thomas McDermott. A Survey of Catholic Literature. Bruce Publishing Company, Milwaukee, 1945.
An informed narrative survey written primarily by Father Brown, who was for many years associated with the famed Central Catholic library in Dublin.

Burr, Nelson R. A Critical Bibliography of Religion in America. Princeton University Press, Princeton, 1961.
A monumental achievement, comprising 2 volumes and almost 1200 pages, this source is highly recommended. Burr, a senior librarian at the Library of Congress, includes many books germane to the study of church-state relations.

Burr, Nelson R. Religion in American Life. Appleton-Century Crofts, New York, 1971.
An updating and addition of many important volumes published in 1960s.

Case, Shirley Jackson, et. al. A Bibliographical Guide to the History of Christianity. New York, 1951.
A remarkable document of source material, including much relevant information on church and state.

Merchant, Harish D. Encounter with Books: A Guide to Christian Reading. Inter Varsity Press, Downers Grove, Illinois, 1971.
A comprehensive Protestant survey of both British and American books in religion.

1

GENERAL BIBLIOGRAPHIES

O'Rourke, William T. Library Handbook for Catholic Students. Bruce
Publishing Company, Milwaukee, 1935.
A partially annotated guide to a wide ranging field of reference
materials.

Regis, Sister M., editor. The Catholic Bookman's Guide. Hawthorn,
New York, 1962.
A literate and comprehensive look at thousands of important Catholic
volumes, with some relevant church-state material. Many specialists
contributed to this outstanding volume.

Religious Reading: An Annual Guide. Consortium Press, Washington, D.C.,
1975.
First of a projected annual series, this is a welcome addition to
the reference shelf. Contains mostly annotated notes on all (or
almost all) British and American religious books for 1973.

Chapter II
CHURCH-STATE RELATIONS: HISTORICAL DEVELOPMENT

In this chapter we consider the books which treat of certain church-state relations in a general or theoretical sense. Books in this area generally take either the separationist or accommodationist line in regard to the proper roles between church and state. Included also are books of an historical nature, tracing the interaction between church and state through various periods of western history from the early church through about the mid-nineteenth century. Primary emphasis is placed on church and state in the United States from the colonial days to the present. The last section of this chapter consists of books dealing with other nations, particularly England and Ireland. There is a representative and selective sample of books for other nations which have been published in English during the last century or so.

A. Historical Development, with Special Reference to United States

Acton, Lord. Essays on Church and State. Dover Publications, New York, 1952. (edited with an introduction by Douglas Woodruff)
Scintillating essays on the relations between church and state throughout history by one of England's greatest historians.

Antieau, Chester James. Freedom from Federal Establishment. Bruce, Milwaukee, 1964.
Author interprets church-state separation to mean a minimum of federal involvement in religious questions and a bulwark against favoritism toward any one religion, but not religion in general.

Antieau, Chester James, et. al. Religion Under the State Constitutions. Central Book, Brooklyn, 1965.
A study of the Institute for Church-State Law at Georgetown University.

Barth, Karl. Church and State. Student Christian Movement, London, 1939.
The preeminent Protestant theologian's views of the jurisdictions of the sacred and the secular.

Batten, Samuel Zane. The Christian State. Griffith and Rowland, Philadelphia, 1909.
A consideration of the Christian Commonwealth and its relevance to a secular world.

Bennett, John C. Christians and the State. Scribners, New York, 1958.
A liberal Protestant view which embodies an accommodationist or cooperationist rather than separationist orientation.

Beth, Loren P. American Theory of Church and State. University of Florida, Gainesville, 1958.
An evaluation and interpretation of the parameters within which U.S. civil and sacral institutions function.

CHURCH-STATE RELATIONS: HISTORICAL DEVELOPMENT

Bevan, Wilson Lloyd. Gospel and Government; the Development of the
    Christian State. Church Missions House, New York, 1914.
    Historical approach.

Black, Hugh. Christ or Caesar? Revell, New York, 1938.
    A conservative Protestant study of the ancient dilemma.

Brown, Wilham Adams. Church and State in Contemporary America.
    Scribners, New York, 1936.
    An analysis of major church-state problems with primary emphasis on
    religious pressure groups.

Cadman, S. Parkes. Christianity and the State. Macmillan, New York, 1924.
    Affirms the belief that ethical and political obligations can be
    reconciled most equitably in a society which separates religion and
    government, thereby granting impetus to the church's prophetic role
    in society.

Coler, Bird Sim. Two and Two Make Four. Beattys, New York, 1914.
    A highly original history of church-state relations.

Cornelison, Isaac A. The Relation of Religion to Civil Government in
    the U.S.A. Putnams, New York, 1895.
    A reasoned and compelling defense of American voluntarism and
    separation which have strengthened, in the author's view, the
    churches' moral vision and ethical sensitivity.

Crapsey, Algernon Sidney. Religion and Politics. Thomas Whittaker,
    New York, 1905.
    Despite the title, this is a collection of lectures on church-state
    relations, from the theoretical to practical historical events,
    including two essays on the teachings of Jesus concerning the state.

Cullmann, Oscar. The State in the New Testament. Scribners, New York, 1956.
    An interpretation of church-state relations in the light of classical
    Protestant theology.

Cummins, Richard J., ed. Catholic Responsibility in a Pluralistic Society.
    Catholic University, Washington, D.C., 1961.
    Essays on controversial church-state issues.

Cunningham, William. Christianity and Politics. Houghton Mifflin, Boston,
    1915.
    The 1914 Lowell lectures, including a general discussion of church-
    state relations and treatment of war and religion.

Curtis, Lionel. Civitas Dei; the Commonwealth of God. Macmillan,
    1934, 1938 revised.
    Shows how concept of Christendom developed through the centruies.

CHURCH-STATE RELATIONS: HISTORICAL DEVELOPMENT

Dawson, Christopher. Religion and the Modern State. Sheed and Ward, London, 1935.
A British Roman Catholic historian's remarkable study, much of which is still germane.

Dawson, Joseph Martin. America's Way in Church, State and Society. Macmillan, New York, 1953.
a paean to America's unique understanding of the separate roles played by religion and government.

Dawson, Joseph Martin. Separate Church and State Now. Richard P. Smith, New York, 1948.
A call for a reaffirmation of the strict separation principle in American law and government.

Dobbins, Gaines Stanley. Can a Religious Democracy Survive? Revell, New York, 1941.
A Southern Baptist view of the limitations of achieving a Christian democracy.

Eckenrode, H. J. Separation of Church and State in Virginia. Richmond, 1910.
A sympathetic assessment of those forces and elements which achieved in late Eighteenth century Virginia a disconnection between the civil and religious authorities.

Ehler, Sidney and John B. Morrall, eds. Church and State Through the Centuries. Newman Press, Westminster, Maryland, 1954.
A wide ranging compilation of secular and ecclesiastical documents on the relationship between church and state from the beginnings of the Middle Ages to the mid-Twentieth Century. Commentaries place the documents in historical context.

Figgis, John Neville. Churches in the Modern State. Longmans, London, 1914. (reprint by Russell and Russell, New York, 1973)
Four scholarly lectures on "the free church in the free state" concept and the Res Publica Christiana.

Foster, Finley Milligan. Church and State, their Relations Considered. Peerless, New York, 1940.
Thoughtful essay.

Foster, Paul. Two Cities; a Study of Church-State Conflict. Newman, Westminster, 1955.
The inherent conflict between two jurisdictions considered.

Fox, Henry Watson. Christianity in Politics. John Murray, London, 1925.
How moral and ethical views can influence secular decisions.

CHURCH-STATE RELATIONS: HISTORICAL DEVELOPMENT

Gavin, Frank. Seven Centuries of the Problem of Church and State.
Princeton University Press, Princeton, 1938.
Outstanding historical work, still worthy of careful study by students.

Geffcken, H. Church and State. 2 vols. London, 1877.
Rather Victorian view but scholarly.

Giannella, Donald A., ed. Religion and the Public Order. University of
Chicago, Chicago, 1964. Cornell University, Ithaca, 1969.
Several provocative articles on civil disobedience, the military
chaplaincy, the Amish and compulsory school laws, and public subsidy
of religious institutions. Produced by Villanova University's
Institute of Church and State.

Gladstone, William E. The State in its Relations with the Church.
John Murray, London, 1839.
A classic defense of the concept of religious establishment and a
Christian state.

Greene, Evarts Boutell. Religion and the State: The Making and Testing
of an American Tradition. New York University, New York, 1941.
A carefully documented study of "America's way" in church and state
in contrast to various church-state unions and accommodations in
the Old World. Stresses the revolutionary uniqueness of the U.S.
approach.

Greenslade, Stanley Lawrence. Church and State from Constantine to
Theodosius. SCM, London, 1954.
Important study of a crucial era in the development of church-state
relations.

Haas, John A. W. The Problem of the Christian State. Stratford, Boston,
1928.
The complexities and difficulties of conforming any secular state to
Christian principles.

Hanley, Thomas O'Brien. The American Revolution and Religion. Consortium
Press, Washington, D.C., 1971.
Slightly misnamed, this volume depicts church-state relations,
religious liberty problems and interfaith conflict in Maryland from
the 1640s to about 1830. Reveals the massive discriminatory provisions against Catholics after the formal Anglican establishment in
1689.

Hardon, John A. Christianity in the Twentieth Century. Doubleday, Garden
City, 1971.
Excellent survey with a chapter solely devoted to "church and state".

Hill, Bennett D., ed. Church and State in the Middle Ages. Wiley, New
York, 1970.
History cum documentary.

6

CHURCH-STATE RELATIONS: HISTORICAL DEVELOPMENT

Hovey, Alvah. Religion and the State, Protection or Alliance? Estes and
   Lauriat, Boston, 1874.
   A consideration of how much assistance the State can or should give
   to religious institutions, including their taxation.

Howe, Mark DeWolfe. Cases on Church and State in the U.S. Harvard
   University, Cambridge, 1952.
   A study of how the civil courts deal with minority rights, education
   and religion, intraecclesiastical adjudications, and churches as
   corporations holding property.

Howe, Mark DeWolfe. The Garden and the Wilderness: Religion and Govern-
   ment in American Constitutional History. University of Chicago,
   Chicago, 1965.
   An accommodationist viewpoint.

Huegli, Albert G., ed. Church and State Under God. Concordia, St. Louis,
   1964.
   Ten essays by specialists on the theological, political and social
   ramifications of church-state interaction. Essential overview which
   ranks among the best theoretical interpretations.

Hurlbut, Elisha P. A Secular View of Religion in the State. J. Munsell,
   Albany, 1870.
   An early separationist viewpoint, including an attack on coerced
   Bible reading in public schools.

Hyma, Albert. Christianity and Politics; a History of the Principles and
   Struggles of Church and State. Lippincott, Philadelphia, 1938.
   Lucid history.

Johnson, Alvin W. and Frank Yost. Separation of Church and State.
   University of Minnesota Press, Minneapolis, 1948.
   The development and preservation of this important legal principle
   through the Everson case.

Jones, Alonzo T. Civil Government and Religion; or Christianity and the
   American Constitution. American Sentinel, Chicago, 1889.
   (Facsimile reprint, 1973, by Atlantic Printers and Publishers
   Sherrington, Quebec, Canada)
   A collection of lectures on the relationship between religion and the
   civil power, delivered by Seventh-day Adventist leader in Minneapolis
   in October 1888. Especially useful when dealing with the so-called
   "Christian Amendment" controversy and the Blair Amendment to require
   uniform Sunday closing throughout the U.S.A.

Kallen, Horace Meyer. Secularism is the Will of God. Twayne, New York,
   1954.
   A polemical defense of the secular state.

CHURCH-STATE RELATIONS: HISTORICAL DEVELOPMENT

Katz, Wilber G. Religion and American Constitutions. Northwestern
University Press, Evanston, 1964.
A study of state constitutions by an authority who argues that state
neutrality toward religion renders aid to parochial schools not
unconstitutional.

Kauper, P. G. Religion and the Constitution. University of Michigan
Press, Ann Arbor, 1962.
A careful legal study of court interpretations of the First
Amendment.

Kerwin, Jerome F. Catholic Viewpoint on Church and State. Hanover House,
Garden City, 1960.
A progressive Catholic interpretation which includes an historical
survey and a discussion of the serious contemporary church-state
issues.

Kik, Jacob Marcellus. Church and State; the Story of Two Kingdoms.
Nelson, New York, 1963.
An Evangelical Protestant interpretation.

Klingberg, Frank Joseph. A Free Church in a Free State, America's Unique
Contribution. Indianapolis, 1947.
An Episcopalian scholar's appreciation of the voluntary principle in
U.S. religious life.

Kninsky, Fred and Joseph Boskin, eds. The Politics of Religion in America.
Beverly Hills, 1968.
Anthology of writings on contentious church-state issues from Alexis
de Tocqueville to Paul Blanshard.

Lecler, Joseph. The Two Sovereignties. Philosophical Library, New York,
1952.
An inquiry into the nature of the dual functions and roles in society
played by the church and state.

Love, Thomas T. John Courtney Murray: Contemporary Church-State Theory.
Doubleday, New York, 1965.
Author attempts to synthesize and evaluate the liberal Catholic
position expounded by Father Murray, particularly his defense of
absolute freedom of conscience.

Lowell, C. Stanley. The Embattled Wall. Americans United, Washington,
D.C., 1966.
An engaging account of the church-state battles and conflicts from
1947 to 1966 by one who was involved in most of them.

Lowell, C. Stanley. The Great Church-State Fraud. Robert B. Luce,
Washington, 1973.
A critical look at the evasions which seem, to the author, to be
eroding the principle of church-state separation in American life.

CHURCH–STATE RELATIONS: HISTORICAL DEVELOPMENT

McGrath, John J. Church and State in American Law. Bruce, Milwaukee, 1962.
A study of the most important legal decisions in U.S. history.

Marshall, Charles C. The Roman Catholic Church in the Modern State. Dodd,
Mead, New York, 1928.
An Episcopalian lawyer critically disects the anti-libertarian
orientation of official Vatican policy.

Meinhold, Peter. Caesar's or God's? The Conflict of Church and State in
Modern Society. Augsburg, Minneapolis, 1962.
A Lutheran view of modern church-state tensions.

Meyer, Jacob C. Church and State in Massachusetts 1750-1833. Cleveland,
1930.
A concise summary of the attempts to disestablish the Congregational
church in Massachusetts. Depicts the hardships Roman Catholics and
other minorities suffered in Colonial and early post-Revolutionary
period.

Moehlman, Conrad H. The American Constitutions and Religion. Berne,
Indiana, 1938.
A thorough documentation.

Moehlman, Conrad H. The Wall of Separation Between Church and State.
Beacon Press, Boston, 1951.
An interpretation and updating of the Jeffersonian-Madisonian
thesis and its contribution to American democracy.

Morgan, Richard E. The Supreme Court and Religion. The Free Press, New
York, 1972.
An absorbing narrative of court decisions relative to the First
Amendment and their effect on American religion.

Morino, Claudio. Church and State in the Teaching of St. Ambrose.
Catholic University of America, Washington, D.C., 1969.
Unique historical-theological study.

Morton, Robert Kemp. God in the Constitution. Cokesbury, Nashville, 1933.
A review of the Constitutional history of church-state relations.

Mueller, William A. Church and State in Luther and Calvin. Broadman,
Nashville, 1954.
A comparative analysis by a profound Baptist thinker.

Murray, Albert Victor. The State and the Church in a Free Society.
Cambridge University, Cambridge, 1958.
The atmosphere of freedom affects both church and state in their
official capacities.

Murray, John Courtney. We Hold These Truths. Sheed and Ward, New York, 1960.
  A truly seminal event in Catholic intellectual life. Murray develops and articulates an American Catholic view of church and state which differs substantially from the official Vatican line. Murray's thought-provoking book may have helped Senator Kennedy's presidential campaign; it was certainly a major factor in the Vatican's approval of a progressive Declaration on Religious Liberty in 1965.

Nichols, James Hastings. Democracy and the Churches. Westminster Press, Philadelphia, 1951.
  A provocative survey of the contributions made by the different Christian churches to the development of democracy and civil liberty.

Norman, Edward R. The Conscience of the State in North America. Cambridge University, Cambridge, 1968.
  Author, a British historian, compares religious liberty in the U.S., Canada, and Britain, and contends that religious dissent led to constitutional separation.

Oaks, Dollin H. The Wall Between Church and State. University of Chicago, Chicago, 1963.
  An accommodationist position.

Osgniach, Augustine John. The Christian State. Bruce, Milwaukee, 1943.
  A Catholic defense of traditional Vatican policy on the rights of the church in a Christian society.

Parker, T. M. Christianity and the State in the Light of History. Harper and Brothers, New York, 1955.
  Excellent historical overview of the early church, Medieval and Reformation periods.

Parsons, W. P. The First Freedom: Considerations on Church and State in the United States. Macmillan, New York, 1948.
  An insightful, meditative reminder of our precious liberties.

Pearson, Andrew F. S. Church and State; Political Aspects of Sixteenth Century Puritanism. Cambridge University, Cambridge, 1928.
  The often overlooked contribution of Puritans to church-state theory.

Penner, Archie. The Christian, the State, and the New Testament. Herald, Scottdale,Pennsylvania, 1959.
  A Mennonite exposition.

Petrie, George. Church and State in Early Maryland. Johns Hopkins, Baltimore, 1892. (reprint Johnson, New York, 1973)
  Brief historical monograph.

Pfeffer, Leo. Church, State and Freedom. Beacon Press, Boston, 1967.
A masterful summary, encompassing the whole range of church-state
interaction, by the dean of American church-state attorneys.

Pfeffer, Leo. Creeds in Competition. Harper and Brothers, New York, 1958.
A brief treatment of virtually every contentious church-state dispute
in the 1950s by an authority who regards the competition between
Protestantism, Catholicism, Judaism and secular humanism to be a
beneficial factor in the creative resolution of tensions. Author shows
how the four major faiths line up on each of the church-state issues.

Pfeffer, Leo. God, Caesar and the Constitution. Beacon Press, Boston, 1975.
A comprehensive look at the status of the "no establishment" and "free
exercise" clauses in American law today.

Prall, William. The State and the Church. T. Whittaker, New York, 1900.
The Baldwin lectures of 1898 by a church historian.

Relton, Herbert Maurice. Religion and the State, a Study of the Problem
of Church and State in the Modern World. Unicorn, London, 1937.
Lectures delivered at St. Paul's Cathedral in 1937.

Robertson, Sir Charles Grant. Religion and the Totalitarian State.
Epworth, London, 1937.
The trials of the churches in hostile societies portrayed.

Rommen, Heinrich Albert. The State in Catholic Thought. B. Herder,
St. Louis, 1945. (reprint Greenwood Press, 1965)
A massive 750 page treatise translated from the German.

Ruff, G. Elson. The Dilemma of Church and State. Muhlenberg Press,
Philadelphia, 1954.
An admirable Lutheran view of this perennial conflict.

Runciman, Sir Steven. The Orthodox Churches and the Secular State.
Auckland University, Auckland, New Zealand, 1971.
Lectures by an eminent scholar on the Eastern Orthodox nations and
their adaptation to Marxism.

Ryan, John A. and F. X. Millar. The State and the Church. Macmillan,
New York, 1922.
A traditionalist Catholic view.

Sanders, Thomas G. Protestant Concepts of Church and State. Holt,
Rinehart, and Winston, New York, 1964.
An attempt to construct a Protestant consensus out of varying
theological interpretations.

CHURCH-STATE RELATIONS: HISTORICAL DEVELOPMENT

Satoli, Archbishop Francis. Loyalty to Church and State. John Murphy,
    Baltimore, 1895.
    Calls on Catholics to support the American system of separation.

Schaff, Philip. Church and State in the United States. Scribners, New
    York, 1888.
    Though written almost a century ago, this is a brilliant commentary
    on the necessity of maintaining religious liberty through church-
    state separation.

Scholes, Frances V. Church and State in New Mexico, 1610-1650.
    University of New Mexico, Albuquerque, 1937.
    The definitive account of a virtually unknown period in early
    American history.

Simpson, Patrick Carnegie. The Church and the State. J. Clarke, London,
    1929.
    A British scholar's analysis.

Smith, Arthur Lionel. Church and State in the Middle Ages. Barnes and
    Noble, New York, 1964.
    Generally adequate history.

Smith, Elwyn A. Church and State in Your Community. Westminster,
    Philadelphia, 1963.
    Brief summary of different Protestant and Catholic views on church-
    state issues through the centuries by a Presbyterian church historian.

Smith, George L. Religion and Trade in New Netherland. Cornell University
    Press, Ithaca and London, 1973.
    The only book-length study of church-state relations and restrictions
    on religious liberty in the Dutch Reformed colony of New Netherland
    1609-1664. Persecution of Quakers and other dissenters marred the
    colony's record but Smith believes that the merchant class tried to
    overrule the clergy and create a more tolerant society.

Stackhouse, Reginald. Christianity and Politics. English University
    Press, London, 1966.
    How church and state can interact with mutual benefit.

Stokes, Anson Phelps. Church and State in the United States. Harper and
    Brothers, New York, 1950. 3 volumes.
    The most scholarly and comprehensive treatment of the subject by a
    distinguished Canon of Washington National Cathedral. A revised
    one volume summary was published in 1964.

Strickland, Reba C. Religion and the State in Georgia in the Eighteenth
    Century. Columbia University, New York, 1939. (reprint AMS, New
    York, 1967)
    Definitive study of a colony about which little is written.

12

CHURCH-STATE RELATIONS: HISTORICAL DEVELOPMENT

Stroup, Herbert. Church and State in Confrontation. Seabury Press, New York, 1967.
An analysis of the inherent tendencies toward conflict in church-state relations.

Sturzo, Luigi. Church and State. University of Notre Dame Press, Notre Dame, Indiana, 1962. 2 volumes. (reprint)
The founder of Italy's Popular Democratic Party, a forerunner of the Christian Democrats, eloquently argues for more democracy in both church and state and a firm separation between the two entities.

Swancara, Frank. The Separation of Religion and Government. Truth Seeker Company, New York, 1950.
A reasoned defense of separation by a prominent rationalist. Includes an extensive appendix of primary source documents.

Syme, Eric. A History of SDA Church-State Relations in the United States. Pacific Press, Mountain View, California, 1973.
The first full length study of how the small Seventh-day Adventist Church has responded to such church-state issues as Sunday law enforcement, temperance, bearing of arms, ecumenism and government funding of religious institutions. One chapter describes the founding of the Religious Liberty Association.

Temple, William. Christianity and the State. Macmillan, London, 1928.
A future Archbishop of Canterbury surveys the historic theories of the two realms.

Thompson, J. P. Church and State in the United States. Boston, 1873.
A scholarly German clergyman wrote this book to interpret the American method of resolving church-state disputes to a German audience. It was simultaneously published in Berlin and translated into English. It is overwhelmingly sympathetic, regarding the U.S. as the ideal pattern for Europe to emulate because "religious liberty is everywhere [in the U.S.] recognized as an absolute personal right."

Thomson, D. E. The Relations of Church and State. Toronto, 1915.
General introduction.

Tierney, Brian. The Crisis of Church and State, 1050-1300. Prentice-Hall, Englewood Cliffs, 1964.
A historical narrative of the developing union of church and state in the High Middle Ages.

Tussman, Joseph. The Supreme Court on Church and State. Oxford University Press, New York, 1962.
The major court rulings from the earliest days until 1953 speak for themselves in this valuable reference work.

CHURCH-STATE RELATIONS: HISTORICAL DEVELOPMENT

Van Dusen, Henry P., ed. Church and State in the Modern World. Harper
and Brothers, New York, 1937.
A symposium on many aspects of church-state relations between the
two World Wars.

Vidler, Alexander R. The Orb and the Cross. SPCK, London, 1945.
A brilliant study of "Christianity and Statesmanship" with particular
reference to Prime Minister William E. Gladstone.

Waring, Luther Hess. The Political Theories of Martin Luther. Kennikat,
Port Washington, New York, 1968.
Important for an understanding of how Lutheran nations solved the
church-state conflict.

Weeks, Stephen Beauregard. Church and State in North Carolina. Johns
Hopkins, Baltimore, 1893. (reprint Johnson, New York, 1973)

Werline, Albert Warwick. Problems of Church and State in Maryland during
the Seventeenth and Eighteenth Centuries. College Press, South
Lancaster, Massachusetts, 1948.

Wilson, John Frederick, ed. Church and State in American History. Heath,
Boston, 1965.
A collection of primary and secondary source material from Colonial
days to 1963.

Wolf, Donald J. Toward Consensus; Catholic-Protestant Interpretations of
Church and State. Doubleday Anchor, New York, 1968.
A number of irenic ecumenists discuss the growing convergence of
accommodationist thinkers, Protestant and Catholic.

Wood, Arthur. The Christian World State. Independent, London, 1949.
The role Christianity can or should play in world affairs.

Wood, James Edward. Church and State in Scripture, History and Constitutional Law. Baylor University, Waco, 1958.
A classic articulation of the Baptist-Separatist view.

Woodruff, Douglas. Church and State. Hawthorn, New York, 1961.
An historical survey from the Fourth Century to the present by a
noted English Catholic.

Zabel, Orville H. God and Caesar in Nebraska. University of Nebraska,
Lincoln, 1955.
A discussion of the church-state implications of the Meyer v. Nebraska
case decided by the U.S. Supreme Court in 1923.

Zollmann, Carl Frederich Gustav. American Church Law. St. Paul, 1933.
An exhaustive compilation of 2,500 cases and judicial decisions
dealing with religion and the law.

B. Historical Development, Other Nations

1. Europe—General

Einaudi, Mario and Francois Goguel. Christian Democracy in Italy and
     France. University of Notre Dame, 1952. (reprint Archon, Hamden,
     1969)
     Excellent study.

Evans, Robert P. Let Europe Hear. Moody, Chicago, 1963.
     A survey of religious conditions in every Western European nation,
     marred by a fundamentalist Protestant bias which sees all historic
     churches as essentially evil.

Fitzsimmons, M. A., ed. The Catholic Church Today: Western Europe.
     University of Notre Dame, Notre Dame and London, 1969.
     A collection of stimulating essays on Catholicism in fourteen
     West European nations.

Fogarty, Michael P. Christian Democracy in Western Europe 1820-1953.
     University of Notre Dame Press, Notre Dame, Indiana, 1957.
     The definitive study of Catholic and Protestant political parties
     in Nineteenth and Twentieth Century Europe. Essential for an
     understanding of religious influences on politics.

Guilday, Peter, ed. The Catholic Church in Contemporary Europe, 1919-1931.
     P. J. Kenedy, New York, 1932.
     A splendid two-volume collection of papers of the American Catholic
     Historical Association.

Helmreich, Ernst Christian, ed. A Free Church in a Free State?; The
     Catholic Church, Italy, Germany, France, 1864-1914. Heath, Boston,
     1964.

Herman, S. W. Report from Christian Europe. Friendship Press, New York,
     1953.
     Problems of postwar reconstruction portrayed.

Isaacson, Charles Stuteville. Rome in Many Lands. Religious Tract Society,
     London, 1903.
     Critical but scholarly study of Roman Catholic political influence
     throughout Europe.

Keller, Adolf. Christian Europe Today. Harper, New York, 1942.
     Not as good as previous volumes but contains useful information of
     church-state conditions in Nazi-occupied and Allied Europe.

Keller, Adolf. Church and State on the European Continent. Epworth,
     London, 1936.
     Definitive, informed analysis of church-state relations in each country
     just before the Holocaust.

CHURCH-STATE RELATIONS: HISTORICAL DEVELOPMENT

Keller, Adolf. Protestant Europe. New York and London, 1928.
    A Swiss Protestant scholar surveys Protestant cultural and political
    life in every country and includes much useful information on inter-
    faith conversions, tensions and misunderstanding in the 1920s.
    He also deals with problems of religious discrimination in many lands.

Mols, Hans, ed. Western Religion. Mouton Publishers, The Hague, 1972.
    A superb compendium of articles on religious sociology and demography
    for every European country except Rumania. (Canada, Australia and
    the U.S.A. are also included) Contains considerable information on
    church-state interaction and religious discrimination.

2. England and Scotland

Amherst, W. J. The History of Catholic Emancipation. Kegan Paul, London,
    1886.
    Very readable account.

Beck, George Andrew, ed. The English Catholics, 1850-1950. Burns and
    Oates, London, 1950.
    An unsurpassed anthology of writings by experts on the growth of
    Roman Catholicism in Britain. Contains much useful information on
    education and religious liberty problems.

Brown, Thomas. Church and State in Scotland. Macniven and Wallace,
    Edinburgh, 1891.
    A narrative of the pivotal years in Scottish history, 1560 to 1843,
    when the present church-state patterns were being fashioned.

Camm, Dom Bede. Lives of the English Martyrs. Longmans Green, London, 1914.
    A classic two-volume study of the English Roman Catholic martyrs.

Catholic Emancipation, 1829 to 1929. (essays by various writers) Longmans,
    Green, New York and London, 1929.
    Varied essays on Catholic progress.

Cruickshank, Marjorie. Church and State in English Education, 1870 to the
    Present Day. Macmillan, London, 1963.
    Fine historical summary.

Cusack, M. J. Revolution and War, or Britain's Peril and Her Secret Foes.
    Allen and Unwin, London, 1913.
    Anti-Papal polemic.

Donaldson, Gordon. Scotland: Church and Nation Through Sixteen Centuries.
    Barnes and Noble, New York, 1973.
    A concise but splendid overview of church-state relations throughout
    Scotland's turbulent history.

16

Galton, Arthur. Our Attitude Towards English Roman Catholics and the
    Papal Court. Elliot Stock, and the Imperial Protestant Federation,
    London, 1902.
    Short but factual account of England's relations with the Papacy
    from the Seventh Century to 1900.

Garbett, Cyril. Church and State in England. Macmillan, New York, 1950.
    A historical survey containing much useful information for an
    understanding of Colonial America's religious establishments as
    well as England's.

Gwatkin, Henry Melvill. Church and State in England to the Death of
    Queen Anne. Longmans, London, 1917.
    Useful and documented.

Harney, Martin P. Magnificent Witnesses. Daughters of St. Paul, Boston,
    1970.
    Brief biographies of the forty Roman Catholic martyrs from England
    and Wales who were canonized by Pope Paul in 1970.

Henriques, Ursula. Religious Toleration in England 1787-1833. University
    of Toronto Press, Toronto, 1961.
    The struggle for Catholic emancipation depicted.

Horne, A. Sinclair. In the Steps of the Covenanters. Scottish Reformation
    Society, 17 George IV Bridge, Edinburgh EH1 1ER, 1974.
    A guide to the shrines of religious martyrs in Scotland. A one-of-its-
    kind publication.

Horne, A. Sinclair. Torchbearers of the Truth. Scottish Reformation
    Society, Edinburgh, 1969.
    A concise, well written introduction to the battle for religious
    freedom in seventeenth century Scotland.

Huxtable, John. Church and State in Education. Religious Education Press,
    Wallington, Surrey, 1960.
    A consideration of religious education in British schools.

Jordan, Wilbur K. The Development of Religious Toleration in England.
    George Allen and Unwin Ltd., London. 4 volumes, 1936-1940.
    One of the best accounts available.

McClelland, Vincent Alan. English Roman Catholics and Higher Education,
    1830-1903. Oxford University Press, Oxford and London, 1973.
    Certainly the standard work on a relatively little-known subject,
    this work is exceptionally valuable.

Montagu, Lord Robert. Recent Events and a Clue to Their Solution.
    London, 1886.
    Strongly fearful of increasing Roman Catholic political influence
    in the realm.

CHURCH-STATE RELATIONS: HISTORICAL DEVELOPMENT

Murphy, James. Church, State and Schools in Britain, 1800-1970.
    Routledge and Kegan Paul, London and Boston, 1971.
    The definitive study, absolutely essential to all students of this
    complex subject.

Norman, E. R. Anti-Catholicism in Victorian England. Barnes and Noble,
    New York, 1968.
    The definitive study, by a brilliant British historian, this volume
    also contains twenty primary source documents of addresses, rallies,
    papers, and government inquiries, showing religious strife in
    Victoria's heyday.

Paton, James. British History and Papal Claims. 2 volumes. Hodder
    and Stoughton, London, 1893.
    A massive, heavily documented study of relations between the Vatican
    and the British government from the Norman Conquest to 1892. Relies
    heavily on official Parliamentary reports.

Pawley, Bernard and Margaret. Rome and Canterbury through Four Centuries.
    Seabury, New York, 1975.
    Absolutely splendid history. Will remain standard for years to come.

Philpot, J. C. The Advance of Popery in this Country. Third edition
    with additional chapters by S. F. Paul. Gospel Standard Publications,
    London, 1965.
    Revision and updating of a controversial 1869 tract which warned of
    growing Roman Catholic influence in the political life of the realm.
    Despite the rather lurid title, most of the book is factually
    accurate and well documented.

Sacks, Benjamin. The Religious Issue in the State Schools of England and
    Wales, 1902-1914. University of New Mexico, Albuquerque, 1961.
    The crucial period before massive government assistance was granted
    to religious schools.

Scott, George. The RCs: A Report on Roman Catholics in Britain Today.
    Hutchinson, London, 1967.
    Fascinating, Guntherian journalistic portrait which considers the
    remaining vestiges of social and legal discrimination and also
    considers the question of a Catholic Prime Minister.

Stoneham, Edward T. The Sussex Martyrs. Henry E. Walter, Ltd., Worthing,
    England, 1973.
    A vivid reminder of the Marian persecutions.

Sykes, N. Church and State in England in the Eighteenth Century.
    Cambridge University Press, Cambridge, 1954.

CHURCH-STATE RELATIONS: HISTORICAL DEVELOPMENT

Thurston, Herbert. No Popery; Chapters on Anti-Papal Prejudice. Longmans
   Green, London and New York, 1930.
   Essays on anti-Roman Catholicism in British history.

Upward, Allen. Treason: Showing How a Roman Catholic Mary III was
   Proclaimed Queen on the Death of Victoria. Tyndall, London, 1903.
   Inflammatory account.

Walsh, Walter. The Secret History of the Oxford Movement. Swan
   Sonnenschein, London, 1898.
   An Evangelical Anglican's expose of the Catholic movement in the
   Church of England, which he believes will lead to the destruction
   of civil and religious liberty and eventual reunion with Rome.

Wilcox, J. D., J. A. Kensit and P.H. Rand. Contending for the Faith.
   Protestant Truth Society, 184 Fleet Street, London EC1, 1962.
   A fascinating history of the Protestant Truth Society from its
   founding in 1897 to 1962. A first-hand account of anti-Papal
   agitation in England and an insight into the extremist Protestant
   mind.

Wuerl, Donald W. The Forty Martyrs. Our Sunday Vistor, Huntington,
   Indiana, 1971.
   Brief sketches of the lives of forty English and Welsh Roman
   Catholic martyrs who died for their faith between 1535 and 1679.
   Contains the canonization homily of Pope Paul VI, given at St. Peter's
   in 1970.

3. Ireland and Northern Ireland

Adams, Michael. Censorship: The Irish Experience. University of
   Alabama, Tuscaloosa, 1968.
   The definitive book-length study of clerically inspired book
   censorship in Ireland.

Akenson, Donald Harman. Education and Enmity: The Control of Schooling
   in Northern Ireland, 1920-1950. David and Charles, Newton Abbott,
   1973. Barnes and Noble, New York, 1973.
   Definitive study of sectarianism in Ulster education.

Ashton, Lord. The Unknown Power Behind the Irish Nationalist Party --
   Its Present Work and Criminal History. London, 1908.
   Blames Roman Catholicism for Ireland's troubles.

Barritt, David P. and Charles F. Carter. The Northern Ireland Problem.
   Oxford University, New York, 1962 (1972 revised).
   Outstanding, impartial account.

CHURCH–STATE RELATIONS: HISTORICAL DEVELOPMENT

Barritt, D. P. and A. Booth. Orange and Green: A Quaker Study of Community Relations in Northern Ireland. Northern Friends Peace Board, Yorks, 1972.
Fine study of options and alternatives available to peaceful majority.

Blanshard, Paul. The Irish and Catholic Power. Beacon, Boston, 1953. (reprint Greenwood, Westport, Connecticut, 1972)
Critical study of a "priest-ridden" society (in the author's view). Well documented.

Bleakley, David. Peace in Ulster. Mowbrays, Oxford, 1972.
Prominent Ulster politician describes efforts toward reconciliation by several Catholic and Protestant organizations.

Bowen, Desmond. Souperism: Myth or Reality? A Study of Catholics and Protestants during the Great Famine. Mercier, Cork, 1970.
An important historical study of Protestant-Catholic conflict in Ireland from about 1800 to 1850. The author is an Irish Anglican who concludes that the Protestant-inspired "Second Reformation" attempt to convert Roman Catholics was not noticeably successful, nor did the Protestants engage in unconscionable activities to "starve" Catholics into conversion.

Boyd, Andrew. Holy War in Belfast. Anvil Books, Tralee, 1969.
Vivid, depressing account of Ulster's heritage of religious bigotry.

Carson, William A. Ulster and the Irish Republic. William W. Clelard, Belfast, 1956.
A defense of Ulster Protestants and their role in helping the Allied cause in World War II.

Corkey, William. Episode in the History of Protestant Ulster. Belfast, 1959.
Definitive account of Protestant demands for religious instruction in Ulster state schools.

Deutsch, Richard R. Northern Ireland 1921-1974: A Select Bibliography. Garland, New York and London, 1975.
An excellent bibliography on Northern Ireland's tragic history.

Dewar, M. W., et. al. Orangeism. Grand Orange Lodge of Ireland, Belfast, 1967.
Three appreciative essays on the Orange Order and its role in Irish religious and political history.

Dill, Edward M. The Mystery Solved, or Ireland's Miseries. The Grand Cause and Cure. Johnstone and Hunter, Edinburgh, 1852.
A Presbyterian cleric's indictment of Rome.

CHURCH-STATE RELATIONS: HISTORICAL DEVELOPMENT

Dillon, Martin and Denis Lehane. *Political Murder in Northern Ireland.*
    Penguin, Harmondsworth, 1973.
    Horrifying accounts of religious slaughter in Ulster 1971-1972.

Feeney, John. *John Charles McQuaid: The Man and the Mask.* Mercier,
    Cork, 1974.
    Brief, interesting biography of a reactionary Roman Catholic prelate
    whose anti-Protestantism made him something of a Catholic Paisley.

Fennell, Desmond. *The Changing Face of Catholic Ireland.* Corpus,
    Washington, D. C., 1968.
    Rather favorable account by an Irish journalist for German Catholic
    press.

Fraser, Morris. *Children in Conflict.* Secker and Warburg, London, 1973.
    Moving case for religious integration of Ulster's schools.

Greer, John. *A Questioning Generation.* Church of Ireland Board of
    Education, Belfast, 1972.
    Important critique of religion courses in Ulster's state schools.

Gray, Tony. *The Orange Order.* Bodley Head, London, 1972.
    Exciting, generally unfavorable account.

Harris, Rosemary. *Prejudice and Tolerance in Ulster.* Manchester
    Univeristy, Manchester, 1972.
    Academic study.

His Bible and His Gun. Belfast, 1912.
    A defense of Ulster Protestants, published anonymously.

Hocking, Joseph. *Is Home Rule Rome Rule?* London, n.d.
    Concludes that it is.

Hurley, Michael, ed. *Irish Anglicanism 1869-1969.* Allen Figgis, Dublin,
    1970.
    A superb anthology on church-state relations, religious conflict and
    education problems in Ireland by a galaxy of prominent authorities.

Jeffery, Frederick. *Methodism and the Irish Problem.* Methodist Conference,
    Newcastle, 1973.
    A brief survey of Methodists in Irish history and their involvement
    in the recent troubles.

MacVeagh, Jeremiah. *Religious Intolerance Under Home Rule.* London,
    Irish Press Agency, n.d.
    Anti-clerical orientation.

CHURCH-STATE RELATIONS: HISTORICAL DEVELOPMENT

McCarthy, Michael J. F. The Nonconformist Treason. William Blackwood, Edinburgh and London, 1912.
The famous anti-clerical accuses Protestant nonconformists of selling out to Rome. Valuable chapters on mixed marriage conflicts after the Ne Temere decree of 1908.

McCarthy, Michael J. F. Priests and People in Ireland. Hodges, Figgis and Company, Dublin, 1902.
Accuses the clergy of subjugating the Irish Catholic people.

McCarthy, Michael J. F. Rome in Ireland. Hodder & Stoughton, London, 1904.
Savage critique of clericalism by a highly unorthodox Catholic of exceptional literary talent.

Manhattan, Avro. Religious Terror in Ireland. Paravision, London, 1971.
Militant defense of Ulster Protestants.

Marrinan, Patrick. Paisley, Man of Wrath. Anvil, Tralee, 1973.
The only full-length biography of the firebrand extremist. Critical.

Menendez, Albert J. The Bitter Harvest: Church and State in Northern Ireland. Robert B. Luce, Washington, D.C., 1974.
An investigation of the origin and roots of religious hatred, with considerable documentary material.

Mescal, John. Religion in the Irish System of Education. Clonmore and Reynolds, Dublin, 1957.
The importance of religion bared.

Miller, David W. Church, State and Nation in Ireland, 1848-1921. University of Pittsburgh, Pittsburgh, 1973.
The definitive study of the churches' role in the development of Irish education.

Murphy, Patrick. Popery in Ireland. London, 1865.
Anti-Papal polemic.

Rose, Richard. Governing Without Consensus. Beacon, Boston, 1971
First rate study.

Ryan, W. P. The Pope's Green Island. Small and Maynard, London, 1912.
Liberal Catholic journalist's unfavorable portrait.

Senior, Hereward. Orangeism in Ireland and Britain 1795-1836. Routledge and Kegan Paul, London, 1966. Ryerson, Toronto, 1966.
Definitive study of the foundation of the Orange Order and the backlash against Catholic Emancipation.

Sheehy, Michael. Is Ireland Dying?: Culture and the Church in Modern
    Ireland. Taplinger, New York, 1969.
    A devastating expose of the deleterious effects of clericalism on
    Irish creativity.

Southern Ireland, Church or State? Ulster Unionist Council, Belfast, n.d.
    (1951)
    Full documentary account of the "Mother and Child" affair which
    compelled Dr. Noel C. Browne to relinquish his cabinet post because
    of clerical interference in politics.

Streeter, Philip. Ireland's Hope. Logos, Plainfield, New Jersey, 1973.
    An attempted solution to Ulster's turmoil.

Target, G. W. Unholy Smoke. Eerdmans, Grand Rapids, 1969.
    Vivid account of the terrible violence of August 1969 by a
    Protestant who sympathizes with the Catholics.

Wells, Ronald A. and Brian S. Mawhinney. Conflict and Christianity in
    Northern Ireland. Eerdmans, Grand Rapids, 1975.
    Adequate introduction to religious roots of Ulster conflict.

Warren, J. The Biretta Blight. J. K. Mitchell, Dublin, 1914.
    A Protestant attack on Catholic clericalism.

Whyte, John H. Church and State in Modern Ireland, 1923-1970. Gill and
    Macmillan, Dublin, 1971.
    The definitive history by a careful scholar at Queens University.

4. Germany

Conway, John S. The Nazi Persecution of the Churches, 1933-1945.
    London and New York, 1968.
    An excellent book based primarily on primary spurce documents of
    germane government records and archives.

Duncan-Jones, A. S. The Struggle for Religious Freedom in Germany.
    London, 1938.
    Depressing account of Nazi tyranny.

Harcourt, Robert d' The German Catholics. London, 1939.
    Portrait of a disheartened, divided community.

Helmreich, Ernst Christian. Religious Education in German Schools: an
    Historical Approach. Harvard University, Cambridge, 1959.
    The definitive account; essential reading.

CHURCH-STATE RELATIONS: HISTORICAL DEVELOPMENT

Lewy, Guenther. The Catholic Church and Nazi Germany. McGraw-Hill,
New York, 1964.
A devastating analysis of the support given Hitler by many German
Catholics, clerical and lay.

Macfarland, C. S. The New Church and the New Germany: A Study of Church
and State. New York, 1934.
Danger signals to Germany's churches.

Martin, Hugh, et. al. Christian Counterattack: Europe's Churches Against
Nazism. Student Christian Movement, London, 1943.
A survey of anti-Nazi heroism by European Christians of all faiths
in fourteen nations. Excellent.

Mason, John Brown. Hitler's First Foes; a Study in Religion and Politics.
Minneapolis, 1936.
Shows how many courageous Christians opposed Hitlerism.

Micklem, Nathaniel. National Socialism and the Roman Catholic Church.
Oxford University, Oxford and London, 1937.
A favorable portrait of a church being persecuted by the Hitler
regime by one who was generally a critic of Rome.

Persecution of the Catholic Church in the Third Reich; Facts and Documents
Translated from the German. (anonymous). London, 1940.
Documentary evidence.

Power, Michael. Religion in the Reich. Longmans, Green, New York,
London, 1939.
The varied religious complexion of Hitler's Germany.

Spotts, Frederic. The Churches and Politics in Germany. Wesleyan
University, Middletown, 1973.
An exceptionally useful, indeed definitive, study of every aspect
of church-state relations in modern Germany.

Tal, Uriel. Christians and Jews in Germany. Cornell University Press,
Ithaca and London, 1974.
A scholarly study of religion, politics and Christian-Jewish
relations in the strongly Protestant Second Reich, 1870-1914.

Walker, Lawrence D. Hitler Youth and Catholic Youth, 1933-1936. Catholic
University of America, Washington, D.C., 1970.
Important study of church-state antagonism embodied in Hitler's
attempt to abolish all church-related activities and organizations
in the Third Reich.

Zahn, Gordon. German Catholics and Hitler's Wars. Herder and Herder,
New York, 1962.
A Catholic historian and sociologist shows the widespread support for
Hitler among German Catholics.

5. Italy

Binchy, Daniel. Church and State in Fascist Italy. Oxford University
Press, New York, 1941.
A prodigious survey of the ambivalent relations between the Papacy
and Mussolini.

Eager, John Howard. Romanism in its Home. American Baptist Publishing
House, Philadelphia, 1899.
A scholarly critique of clericalism and anti-Protestant discrimination
by a Baptist missionary-resident in Italy.

Garibaldi, Giuseppe. The Rule of the Monk. Harper, New York, 1870.
Italy's great patriot and Risorgimento leader criticizes the Papal
States and the anti-democratic policy of the Papacy.

Giustiniani, L. Papal Rome As It Is. Publication Rooms, Baltimore, 1843.
Expose of conditions in the Papal States by an ex-priest who became
a Lutheran minister.

Halperin, Samuel William. Italy and the Vatican at War. University of
Chicago, Chicago, 1939. (reprint Greenwood, New York, 1968)
An exhaustive study of Vatican policy toward the Italian government
(and vice versa) from the Franco-Prussian War to the death of Pius IX.

Halperin, Samuel William. The Separation of Church and State in Italian
Thought from Cavour to Mussolini. University of Chicago, Chicago, 1937.
(reprint Octagon, New York, 1971)

Jemolo, A. C. Church and State in Italy 1850-1960. Blackwell, Oxford, 1960.
The standard study of the explosive church-state issues from the
Risorgimento to the present.

Robertson, Alexander. The Papal Conquest. Morgan and Scott, London, 1909.
A look at the church's rising political and educational power.

Robertson, Alexander. The Roman Catholic Church in Italy. Morgan and
Scott, London, 1902.
A critical look by a Scottish Presbyterian missionary, resident in
Italy for many years. Sympathetic to the Italian Republic.

Webb, Leicester C. Church and State in Italy, 1947-1957. Melbourne
University Press, Carlton, Victoria, Australia, 1958.
Excellent survey of a critical period.

Webster, R. Christian Democracy in Italy, 1860-1960. London, 1961.
Historical study of the vicissitudes of Christian Democracy.

CHURCH-STATE RELATIONS: HISTORICAL DEVELOPMENT

6. Russia

Anderson, Paul B. People, Church and State in Modern Russia. SCM, London, 1944. Macmillan, New York, 1944. Comprehensive account.

Beeson, Trevor. Discretion and Valour: Religious Conditions in Russia and Eastern Europe. Collins, London, 1974. The most accurate, contemporary study of religious liberty problems and accommodation between church and state in each of the nations of East Europe. Vastly superior to any other works in print.

Bociurkiw, Bohdan R. and John W. Strong. Religion and Atheism in the U.S.S.R. and Eastern Europe. Macmillan, London, 1975. A collection of papers surveying various aspects of religion in Eastern Europe since the Second World War.

Bourdeaux, Michael. Faith on Trial in Russia. Harper and Row, New York, 1971. An international expert on religion in Russia and an Anglican priest who directs Keston College in England surveys the ebb and flow of religious freedom in this vast country.

Bourdeaux, Michael. Patriarch and Prophets: Persecution of the Russian Orthodox Church today. Praeger, New York, 1970. (new edition Mowbrays, Oxford, 1975) A compelling collection of primary source documents revealing widespread repression in the Soviet Union.

Bourdeaux, Michael. The Evidence That Convicted Aida Skipnikova. David C. Cook, Elgin, Illinois, 1973. The trial of a Russian Christian.

Cohen, Richard, ed. Let My People Go. Popular Library, New York, 1971. A portrait of the suffering Jewish community in contemporary Russia.

Conquest, Robert. Religion in the U.S.S.R. Praeger, New York, 1968. Documented and persuasive.

Curtiss, John Shelton. The Russian Church and the Soviet State, 1917-1950. Little, Brown, Boston, 1953. A scholarly analysis of church-state relations during the dark, repressive days of Lenin and Stalin. Invaluable.

Deyneka, Anita and Peter. Christians in the Shadow of the Kremlin. David C. Cook, Elgin, Illinois, 1974. Religious persecution deplored.

CHURCH-STATE RELATIONS: HISTORICAL DEVELOPMENT

Durasoff, Steve. _Pentecost Behind the Iron Curtain._ Logos, Plainfield, New Jersey, 1972.
    The rise of underground Christendom in Soviet Union and Eastern Europe.

Grossu, Sergiu, ed. _The Church in Today's Catacombs._ Arlington House, New Rochelle, 1975.
    Anthology of evidence of religious repression from many Communist lands.

Grunwald, Constantin De. _The Churches and the Soviet Union._ Macmillan, New York, 1962. Hutchinson, London, 1961.
    Complete survey of church-state conflict in Russia by a prodigious scholar.

Hecker, Julius F. _Religion and Communism: A Study of Religion and Atheism in Soviet Russia._ Chapman and Hall, London, 1933.
    The destruction of Christianity in only a decade.

Kolarz, Walter. _Religion in the Soviet Union._ St. Martins, New York, 1961.
    Dramatic panorama.

Marshall, Richard C., et. al., ed. _Aspects of Religion in the Soviet Union, 1917-1967._ University of Chicago, Chicago, 1971.
    Several academics contribute to this excellent survey of the persistence of religion in a hostile environment.

Powell, David E. _Antireligious Propaganda in the Soviet Union._ M.I.T., Cambridge, 1975.
    A thorough survey of Russia's curious freedom to unbelievers contrasted with the lack of free exercise to believers in any religion.

Scheffbuch, Winrich. _Christians under the Hammer and Sickle._ Zondervan, Grand Rapids, 1974.
    The ghettoization of Christian believers.

Shuster, George N. _Religion Behind the Iron Curtain._ Macmillan, New York, 1954.
    An engrossing survey of each Eastern European country during a particularly contentious, divisive era of confrontation between civil and ecclesiastical authorities.

Simon, Gerhard. _Church, State and Opposition in the U.S.S.R._ University of California, Berkeley, 1974. Hurstand Company, London, 1974.
    Deals with creative opposition to the status quo by Christian underground groups who opposed the establishment in both church and state through the centuries. Includes valuable documentary material.

Szezesnick, Bolestow, ed. _The Russian Revolution and Religion._ University of Notre Dame, Notre Dame, 1959.
    A superior collection of primary source documents concerning suppression of religion by the Bolshevik regime from 1917 to 1925. Contains historical essays, appendices and bibliography.

CHURCH-STATE RELATIONS: HISTORICAL DEVELOPMENT

Vins, Georgi. Georgi Vins: Testament from Prison. David C. Cook, Elgin,
    Illinois, 1975.
    Documents smuggled out of a Soviet prison and written by a dissident
    Baptist preacher. A vivid translation by the Centre for the Study
    of Religion and Communism in England.

7. France

Bosworth, William. Catholicism and Crisis in Modern France. Princeton
    University Press, Princeton, 1962.
    The standard study of the reintegration of the church into contem-
    porary French life and culture.

Houghton, Louise Seymour. Handbook of French and Belgian Protestantism.
    Federal Council of Churches, New York, 1919.
    History of Reformed Church in France and its suffering and struggles
    for liberty.

Irving, R. E. Christian Democracy in France. George Allen and Unwin,
    London, 1975.
    Complete survey.

McManners, John. Church and State in France, 1870-1914. Harper, New
    York, 1973.
    Reasonably adequate survey of important epoch, e.g. the separation
    of 1907.

Schram, Stuart R. Protestantism and Politics in France. Imprimerie
    Cofiere and Jugain, Alecon, 1954.
    Unique study of a minority's influence.

8. Spain

Blanshard, Paul. Freedom and Catholic Power in Spain and Portugal.
    Beacon, Boston, 1962.
    Blanshard's critical, probing eye focuses on the reactionary
    ecclesiastical and political tyranny on the Iberian Peninsula.
    A devastating analysis of the pre-ecumenical climate.

Cooper, Norman B. Catholicism and the Franco Regime. Sage, London, 1975.
    Most recent, up-to-date account.

Delpech, Jacques. The Oppression of Protestants in Spain. Beacon,
    Boston, 1955.
    A French Protestant pastor's plea for more religious freedom for
    his brethren.

CHURCH-STATE RELATIONS: HISTORICAL DEVELOPMENT

Gallo, Max. Spain under Franco. Dutton, New York, 1974.
A French journalist's study, concluding that the Roman Catholic
Church has been a main prop of the regime.

Hughey, John D. Religious Freedom in Spain. Broadman, Nashville, 1955.
The ebb and flow of religious freedom throughout Spanish history
vividly portrayed.

Irizarry, Carmen. The Thirty Thousand: Modern Spain and Protestantism.
Holt, Rinehart and Winston, New York, 1966.
A Puerto Rican Catholic journalist, resident in Madrid, surveys
the lot of the Spanish Protestant from Reformation times to the
present. She is indignant at the discrimination against this
tiny minority but reveals their courage and determination, as well
as the new spirit of tolerance among many Spanish Catholics.

Jackson, Gabriel. The Spanish Republic and the Civil War, 1931-1939.
Princeton University, Princeton, 1965.
An admirable study of the Spanish Civil War which includes infor-
mation about church-state conflict.

Lunn, Arnold. Spanish Rehearsal. Sheed and Ward, New York, 1937.
A British Catholic defends the Franco Rebellion and the Catholic
Church, claiming that anticlerical persecution was ignored by the
world's secular press.

Matthews, Herbert L. The Yoke and the Arrows. Braziller, New York, 1957.
Excellent report on Spain by a New York Times specialist. Deals
critically with repression of Protestants and Jews.

Monroy, Juan Antonio. A Defense of Spanish Protestants. Protestant
Truth Society, London, 1966.
Contends that Spansih Protestants are loyal citizens who love their
country but desire true liberty of conscience.

Pattee, Richard. The Religious Question in Spain. National Council of
Catholic Men, Washington, D. C., 1950.
A former American diplomat and specialist in Spanish affairs defends
the Catholic Church in Spain from charges of religious discrimination
against Protestants.

Thierry, Jean Jacques. Opus Dei. Cortland, New York, 1975.
A French journalist's sympathetic assessment of the politico-religious
group which is immensely powerful in Spain.

Vought, Dale G. Protestants in Modern Spain. William Carey Library,
South Pasadena, California, 1973.
The most up-to-date report on the struggle for religious pluralism
and the practical implications of the 1967 Law of Religious Liberty.

CHURCH-STATE RELATIONS: HISTORICAL DEVELOPMENT

Welles, Benjamin. Spain: The Gentle Anarchy. Praeger, New York, 1965.
Excellent study, with considerable material on the Vatican concordat
and church control over education.

9. Canada

Crunican, Paul. Priests and Politicians: Manitoba Schools and the
Election of 1896. University of Toronto Press, 1974.
Crucial election determined by parochial school aid issue. A case
study of religio-political conflict revolving around the aid-to-
church-schools question.

Lupul, Manoly R. The Roman Catholic Church and the North-West School
Question: A Study in Church-State relations in Western Canada,
1875-1905. University of Toronto Press, Toronto, 1974.
A meticulous history of church-state conflict on Canada's frontier,
which reveals the pattern by which parochial schools received
substantial state fudning.

Maloney, John J. Rome in Canada. Columbia Protestant Publications,
Vancouver, 1934.
A critical examination of Roman Catholic political influence in
Canada.

Moir, John S. Church and State in Canada West, 1841-1867. University of
Toronto Press, Toronto, 1959.
Church-state conflict in pre-Dominion days.

Price, Neil G. Education, Religion and Politics in Ontario. Northland
Printers, North Bay, Ontario, 1966.
The "schools controversy" divided Catholics and Protestants in
Ontario for decades.

Religious Education and Moral Development. Ontario Department of Education,
Toronto, 1969.
A report of the Committee on Religious Education in the Public Schools
of the Province of Ontario.

Riddell, W. A. Rise of Ecclesiastical Control in Quebec. New York, 1916.
Most complete account of rise of clericalism in French Canada.

Saunders, Leslie. The Cost of Romanism to the Nation. Canadian Protestant
League, Toronto, 1946.
Accuses Roman Catholic Church of being a fifth column in Protestant
Canada.

Sissons, C. B. Church and State in Canadian Education. Ryerson Press,
Toronto, 1959.
Sober discussion of relevant issues.

30

Weir, George M. The Separate School Question in Canada. Ryerson Press,
Toronto, 1934.
Early account of "parochiaid" dispute Canadian style.

10. Latin America

Bailey, David C. Viva Cristo Rey! University of Texas, Austin and
London, 1974.
A balanced account of church-state conflict in Mexico from 1926
to 1929.

Bonilla, Victor Daniel. Servants of God or Masters of Men? Penguin,
Baltimore, 1972.
Detailed examination of the political and economic influence wielded
by Capuchin Monks in Colombia from 1905 to the present.

Calcott, Wilfred Hardy. Church and State in Mexico 1822-1857. Duke
University, Durham, 1926.
A study of clerical power which led to the confiscation of church
property in 1857.

Holleran, Mary P. Church and State in Guatemala. Columbia University
Press, New York, 1949.
The only English language study available. Author concludes that
close church-state ties have harmed the church's mission.

Howard, George P. Religious Liberty in Latin America. Westminster,
Philadelphia, 1944.
An excellent survey of the varying conditions throughout South and
Central America. Highly critical of Roman Catholic church-state
union.

Kennedy, John J. Catholicism, Nationalism and Democracy in Argentina.
University of Notre Dame, Notre Dame, 1958.
Fascinating account of Peron days.

Macfarland, Charles S. Chaos in Mexico: Conflict of Church and State.
Harper and Brothers, New York, 1935.
A survey of the bitter conflicts.

Mecham, John L. Church and State in Latin America. University of North
Carolina Press, Chapel Hill, 1934. (revised edition 1967)
A definitive study of Hispanic America which has never really been
surpassed.

Mutchler, David. The Church as a Political Factor in Latin America.
Praeger, New York, 1971.
A fact-filled, provocative study by a former Jesuit scholastic who
revealed substantial CIA-church group connection.

CHURCH-STATE RELATIONS: HISTORICAL DEVELOPMENT

Parsons, Wilfred. *Mexican Martyrdom*. Macmillan, New York, 1936.
Author charges that the Catholic Church was fiercely persecuted by
the secular authorities.

Rice, Elizabeth Ann. *The Diplomatic Relations Between the United States
and Mexico as Affected by the Struggle for Religious Liberty in
Mexico, 1925-1929*. Catholic University of America, Washington, D.C.,
1959.
A defense of the Catholic forces in the Mexican conflict plus an
assessment of American policy.

Quirk, Robert E. *The Mexican Revolution and the Catholic Church 1910-1929*.
Indiana University, Bloomington and London, 1973.
An evenhanded review of the serious confrontation between revolutionary
Mexico and the church.

11. Miscellaneous

Gheddo, Piero. *The Cross and the Bo Tree: Catholics and Buddhists in
Vietnam*. Sheed and Ward, New York, 1970.
A study of the religious dimension of the Vietnam conflict by an
informed Italian priest-journalist.

Markowitz, Marvin D. *Cross and Sword: The Political Role of Christian
Missions in the Belgian Congo, 1908-1960*. Hoover Institution Press,
Stanford University, Stanford, California, 1973.
A definitive analysis of the manipulative use of religion for
political ends in Central Africa. Essential reading for specialists.

Truman, Tom. *Catholic Action and Politics*. Merlin, London, 1960.
A documented history of the 1945-1955 attempt by Australia's Catholic
Action to influence the policy direction of the Australian Labour
Party, especially on the issue of state aid to Catholic schools.

Chapter III

DEVELOPMENT OF RELIGIOUS LIBERTY

What Americans call "free exercise" is merely one phase of
religious liberty, though for most other nations it constitutes the common
understanding of the term. Books in this chapter deal with man's struggle
to achieve liberty of conscience. As the struggle for religious liberty
has often been a difficult one, and often subject to many setbacks, one
should also consider the section "martyrdom and persecution" in the following chapter as a cross-reference with this one.

Abbott, Walter, ed. Documents of Vatican II. Association Press, New York,
1966.
Contains the complete English translation of the highly significant
Declaration on Religious Freedom approved by the Council in 1965.

Altfeld, E. Milton. The Jew's Struggle for Religious and Civil Liberty in
Maryland. M. Curlander, Baltimore, 1924.
Excellent account of Eighteenth and early Nineteenth century Maryland.

Augustin, Pius. Religious Freedom in Church and State; a Study in
Doctrinal Development. Helicon, Baltimore, 1966.
A study of Roman Catholic doctrine as it has changed through the
centuries.

Bainton, Roland. The Travail of Religious Liberty. Westminster Press,
Philadelphia, 1951.
Biographical sketches of individuals as varied as Roger Williams and
Torquemada, who were intimately involved in either the furtherance
or repression of religious liberty, by an eminent church historian.

Barr, James. Religious Liberty in the Totalitarian States. Allenson,
London, 1938.
Depressing depiction of repression in Fascist and Communist societies.

Basic Documents Relating to the Religious Clauses of the First Amendment.
Americans United, Silver Spring, 1969.
A collection of primary source documents including Jefferson's
"Letter to the Danbury Baptists" and Madison's "Memorial and
Remonstrance Against Religious Assessments".

Bates, Ernest Sutherland. American Faith. Norton, New York, 1940.
A paean to American concern for freedom of conscience.

Bates, M. Searle. Religious Liberty: An Inquiry. International
Missionary Council, New York, 1945.
A comprehensive, kaleidoscopic survey of both the constitutional
provisions and practical realities in each country of the world.
The author "rates" each area and correlates the degree of liberty
with the predominant religion. Slightly dated but useful.

Blakely, William Addison. American State Papers on Freedom of Religion.
Review and Herald, Washington, D. C., 1943.
Superb compilation; invaluable to scholars.

Blau, Joseph L, ed. Cornerstones of Religious Freedom in America. Beacon Press, Boston, 1949. (revised edition Harper and Row, New York, 1964) A superb primary source anthology of basic documents, court decisions and public statements relating to religious freedom.

Brockunier, Samuel Hugh. The Irrepressible Democrat, Roger Williams. New York, 1940. Sympathetic portrait.

Byrd, Valois. Pioneers of Religious Liberty Convention Press, Nashville, 1963. Primarily Baptist luminaries are considered.

Carlson, C. Emanuel and W. Barry Garrett. Religious Liberty. Convention Press, Nashville, 1964. A fascinating collection of eight case studies in issues relating to religious freedom.

Carlyle, Alexander James. The Christian Church and Liberty. J. Clarke, London, 1924. A plea for liberty within the churches and within professing Christian societies.

Carpenter, Edmund J. Roger Williams. Grafton Press, New York, 1909. Favorable assessment of the famous dissenter.

Carrillo de Albornoz, A. F. The Basis of Religious Liberty. Association Press, New York, 1963. The Secretary of the World Council of Churches' Religious Liberty Department's inquiry into the nature, philosophical base and contemporary relevance of religious freedom. Contains an appendix on the main declarations on religious liberty issued by world religious and political bodies.

Carrillo de Albornoz, A. F. Religious Liberty. Sheed and Ward, New York, 1967. An admiring look at the Second Vatican Council's Declaration on Religious Freedom.

Carrillo de Albornoz, A. F. Roman Catholicism and Religious Liberty. World Council of Churches, Geneva, Switzerland, 1959. A former Spanish Catholic who became a Protestant evaluates the Roman position on full religious liberty. The author headed the Religious Liberty Secretariat of the World Council of Churches for many years and was considerably interested in hopeful signs within Roman Catholicism's attitude to freedom of conscience.

Cobb, Sanford H. The Rise of Religious Liberty in America. New York, 1902. An historical narrative of the long, slow development of religious libertarianism in American civil law. He depicts the cultural influences which created in the U.S. a "unique solution of the world-old problem of church and state - a solution so unique, so far-reaching

and so markedly diverse from European principles as to constitute
the most striking contribution of America to the science of
government". One of the best volumes on the subject.

Constitutional Provisions for Religious Liberty - Federal and State.
Americans United, Washington, D. C., 1967. (introductory commentary
by Franklin C. Salisbury)
A compilation of all statements dealing with religious freedom,
education, church tax exemption and related questions in the
constitutions of each of the states. Presently in process of
revision - new edition planned for 1976.

Crooker, Joseph Henry. The Winning of Religious Liberty. Pilgrim Press,
Boston, 1918.
A summary of the highlights of man's eternal struggle.

Cuninggim, Merrimon. Freedom's Holy Light. Harper and Brothers, New
York, 1955.
An investigation of the Puritan-Calvinist influences on the develop-
ment of religious liberty in the American experience.

Curran, Francis X. Catholics in Colonial Law. Chicago, 1963.
A frightening account of legal prejudice and discrimination against
Catholics in Colonial America.

Dalrymple, Gwynne. The Fight for Freedom. Review and Herald, Washington,
D.C., 1941.
Seventh-day Adventist contributions to the assurance of liberty of
belief.

Davies, Alfred Mervin. Foundations of American Freedom. Abingdon Press,
Nashville, 1955.
A consideration of the central importance of religious liberty in
the framework of other freedoms.

Davies, A. Powell. The Urge to Persecute. Beacon, Boston, 1954.
A trenchant analysis of the persecutory impulse in authoritarian
religions and governments, by an eminent Unitarian pastor and writer.

Dieffenbach, Albert C. Religious Liberty: The Great American Illusion.
New York, 1927.
A revisionist critique which charges that discrimination and prejudice
against minorities render the whole claim of religious freedom invalid.

Doerries, Hermann. Constantine and Religious Liberty. Yale University,
New Haven, 1960.
A vivid and scholarly presentation of a seminal event in Western
cultural history and the problems the "Constantinian Settlement"
bequeathed to future generations.

Easton, Emily. Roger Williams, Prophet and Pioneer. New York, 1930.
Emphasis on Williams' startling and advanced concepts of toleration.

DEVELOPMENT OF RELIGIOUS LIBERTY

Ernst, James Emanuel. Roger Williams, New England Firebrand. New York,
1932.
Objective assessment.

Foote, Henry Wilder. Thomas Jefferson - Champion of Religious Freedom.
Beacon Press, Boston, 1947.
An appraisal of Jefferson's central role in the constitutional
guarantee of the religious liberty Americans now enjoy.

Ford, David B. New England's Struggle for Religious Liberty. Philadelphia,
1896.
Emphasis on Baptist involvement in the move to disestablish the state
churches and create an open society.

Gerson, Noel. The Edict of Nantes. Grosset and Dunlap, New York, 1969.
A rather elementary study of the landmark event in the struggle
for religious freedom.

Gewehr, W. M. The Great Awakening in Virginia. Duke University, Durham,
North Carolina, 1930.
Shows how revivalistic religious movements conflicted with the
established church and, through creative tension, helped to create
religious pluralism.

Hanley, Thomas O'Brien. Their Rights and Liberties: The Beginnings of
Religious and Political Freedom in Maryland. Newman, Westminster,
1959.
A Jesuit historian's very sympathetic assessment of early Catholic
Maryland and its contribution to the development of religious
freedom in America. Contains a good bibliography and a foreword
by Senator Eugene McCarthy.

Hudson, W. S. The Great Tradition of the American Churches. Harper and
Brothers, New York, 1953.
A fascinating study of the voluntary principle in American religion
and its relation to liberty.

Ives, J. Moss. The Ark and the Dove: The Beginning of Civil Religious
Liberties in America. New York, 1936.
A sympathetic assessment of early Catholic Maryland's contribution
to the development of religious freedom.

James, Charles F. Documentary History of the Struggle for Religious
Liberty in Virginia. Lynchburg, Virginia, 1900.
An admirable collection of primary source documents which are of
inestimable value to serious historians of the period.

Janssens, Louis. Freedom of Conscience and Religious Freedom. Alba House,
Staten Island, New York, 1966.
A Catholic defense of absolute religious freedom.

DEVELOPMENT OF RELIGIOUS LIBERTY

Johns, Varney Jay. Forty Centuries of Law and Liberty; a History of the Development of Religious Liberty. Pacific Press, Mountain View, California, 1940.
Vivid panorama.

Johnson, Thomas Cary. Virginia Presbyterians and Religious Liberty in Colonial and Revolutionary Times. Richmond, 1907.
Contends that Presbyterians furnished the most effective leadership in the struggle for religious freedom.

Jones, Alonzo T. The Divine Right of Individuality in Religion; or, Religious Liberty Complete. Battle Creek, Michigan, 1908.
Seventh-day Adventist statement of belief.

Kenny, Denis. The Catholic Church and Freedom. University of Queensland, Brisbane, Australia, 1967.
Urges reevaluation of liberty by Catholics.

King, Henry Melville. Religious Liberty, an Historical Paper. Preston and Rounds, Providence, 1903.
Brief discussion of high points.

Konvitz, Milton R. Fundamental Liberties of a Free People. Cornell University, Ithaca, 1957.
A superb study of the development of religious liberty and its direct relation to other civil liberties.

Konvitz, Milton R. Religious Liberty and Conscience: A Constitutional Inquiry. Viking, New York, 1968.
A study of conscience, the state, and civil disobedience.

Krishnaswami, Arcot. Study of Discrimination in the Matter of Religious Rights and Practices. United Nations, New York, 1960.
Report of a special sub-commission of the United Nations which recommended a covenant of religious liberty for all nations of the world. (Draft of covenant included in appendix.)

Lamb, George R. Tolerance and the Catholic. Sheed and Ward, New York, 1955.
A symposium on religious toleration and Catholic traditions which falls short of the more enlightening studies of John Courtney Murray.

Lasker, Bruno. Religious Liberty and Mutual Understanding. National Conference of Christians and Jews, New York, 1932.
Report of a seminar attended by Prostestants, Catholics and Jews in Washington, D. C. March 7-9, 1932.

Little, Lewis Peyton. Inprisoned Preachers and Religious Liberty in Virginia. J. P. Bell and Company, Lynchburg, 1938.
Interesting account of an appalling event in Colonial history.

DEVELOPMENT OF RELIGIOUS LIBERTY

Locke, John. A Letter on Toleration. (edited by Raymond Klibansky). Clarendon Press, Oxford, 1968.
The most recent reprint of the famous classic with extensive notes and commentaries.

Lowell, C. Stanley and Albert J. Menendez. We Hold These Truths. Americans United Research Foundation, Silver Spring, 1974.
A compilation of historic statements on freedom of conscience and religious liberty from many sources and traditions.

Luzzatti, Luigi, ed. God in Freedom; Studies in the Relations between Church and State. Macmillan, New York, 1930.
Translation of a 1909 Italian study of religious liberty, with supplementary chapters by President William H. Taft.

McIlwane, Henry R. The Struggle of Protestant Dissenters. Baltimore, 1894.
How nonconformist religious groups helped to achieve liberty for future generations.

McLoughlin, William G., ed. Isaac Backus on Church, State and Calvinism. The Belknap Press of Harvard University, Cambridge, 1968.
A collection of pamphlets and addresses on religious liberty by a foremost Colonial Baptist leader whose contribution to the cause of religious freedom is being recognized more each year. Each document is placed in historical context by the editor, who also contributed an excellent introduction.

Marnell, William. The First Amendment: The History of Religious Freedom in America. Doubleday, New York, 1964.
One of the best short histories available.

Miegge, Giovanni. Religious Liberty. Association Press, New York, 1957.
A perceptive assessment by an Italian Waldensian scholar who lived through decades of persecution in his native Italy.

Miller, Perry. Roger Williams, His Contribution to the American Tradition. Bobbs-Merrill, Indianapolis, 1953.
Superior interpretation of Williams' contributions by an eminent historian.

Morgan, Edmund S. Roger Williams: Church and State. Harcourt, Brace and World, New York, 1967.
A philosophical inquiry considered by many historians to be the best study of Williams' thought.

Murray, John Courtney. The Problem of Religious Freedom. Newman, Westminster, 1965.
Sequel to "We Hold These Truths". (See Chapter II)

Northcott, Cecil. Religious Liberty. Macmillan, New York, 1949.
A brief but judicious overview by a well known Englishman.

DEVELOPMENT OF RELIGIOUS LIBERTY

O'Connell, David A. Christian Liberty. Newman, Westminster, 1952.
A moderate Catholic view.

Owen, George Earle. Faith and Freedom; the Problem of Religious Freedom
and the Christian Answer. Philippine Federation of Christian Churches,
Manila, 1953.
Strong plea for absolute liberty.

Patton, Jacob Harris. The Triumph of the Presbytery of Hanover; or,
Separation of Church and State in Virginia. New York, 1887.
Credit is duly given to this Presbyterian group, which began creative
agitation against ecclesiastical establishment in 1773.

Persons, Stow. Free Religion: An American Faith. Yale University, New
Haven, 1947.
A sympathetic appraisal of religious pluralism and independence from
government in American religious history.

Polishook, Irwin H. Roger Williams, John Cotton, and Religious Freedom.
Prentice-Hall, Englewood Cliffs, 1967.
Reflections on early Colonial days.

Power, Francis J. Religious Liberty and the Police Power of the State.
Catholic University, Washington, D.C., 1948.
Study of inevitable conflicts between free exercise and civil
obedience.

Regan, Richard J. American Pluralism and the Catholic Conscience.
Macmillan, New York, 1963.
Defense of religious liberty American style by a Catholic scholar.

Ruffini, Francesco. Religious Liberty. Putnam, New York, 1912.
A magisterial study of man's eternal struggle for freedom of
conscience from pre-Christian days to 1910 by an eminent Italian.
Probably the best historical survey available.

Smith, Elwyn A. Religious Liberty in the United States. Fortress Press,
Philadelphia, 1972.
A concise and lucid historical survey of several major elements in
the development of religious liberty.

Snow, Charles M. Religious Liberty in America. Review and Herald,
Washington, D. C., 1914.
A Seventh-day Adventist statement on the importance of preserving
religious liberty through strict application of the separation
principle.

Straus, Roger Williams. Religious Liberty and Democracy. Willett, Clark
and Company, New York, 1939.
A Jewish scholar's eloquent study of liberty of conscience.

DEVELOPMENT OF RELIGIOUS LIBERTY

Swank, Harold Allen. _The Glory of a Nation_. Greensboro, North Carolina, 1921.
Hails religious freedom as star in American crown.

Thom, W. F. _The Struggle for Religious Freedom in Virginia_. Baltimore, 1900.
A historical survey with primary emphasis on the contributions of Baptists, Presbyterians and other dissenters.

Thorning, Francis Joseph. _Religious Liberty in Transition_. Washington, D. C., 1931.
A systematic analysis of the implementation of the separation principle in the states from 1789 to 1833, when Massachusetts became the last state to disestablish its state church. Author concludes that political opportunism, not sincere religious conviction, brought about the constitutional changes.

Torpey, William G. _Judicial Doctrines of Religious Rights in America_. University of North Carolina, Chapel Hill, 1948.
Careful legal study.

Trueblood, Elton. _Declaration of Freedom_. Harper and Brothers, New York, 1955.
Reflections on America's unique gift of religious liberty by the beloved Quaker theologian.

Van Loon, Hendrik. _Tolerance_. Liveright, New York, 1927. (revised edition 1940)
A widely read "popularizer" of history surveys the whole sweep of man's struggle for the right to think freely. A brilliant case for the defense of freedom of conscience, including a fine chapter on Tom Paine.

Weaver, Rufus W. _Champions of Religious Liberty_. The Sunday School Board of the Southern Baptist Convention, Nashville, 1946.
An historical approach, with emphasis on those men and women and denominations which furthered the goals of religious freedom for all. Strongly Baptist orientation and tone.

Williams, Chester Sidney. _Religious Liberty_. Row, Peterson, New York, 1941.
A textbook-type depiction.

Winslow, Ola Elizabeth. _Master Roger Williams_. New York, 1957.
Elementary level biography.

Wood, H. G. _Religious Liberty Today_. Cambridge University Press, 1949.
A scholarly and perceptive survey of the problem.

Chapter IV

RELIGIOUS CONFLICT

Religious conflict has been part of man's civilization for centuries and has become particularly bitter in the Catholic-Protestant wars which began at the time of the Reformation and have continued through present day Northern Ireland. Books in this chapter include historical treatments of religious conflict plus some examples of polemics associated with inter-faith conflict. The second part of this chapter will deal with martyrdom and persecution for the cause of religion, which have been a prominent feature of religious life in western civilization.

A. Historical

Balmes, Jaime Luciana. European Civilization: Protestantism and Catholicity compared in their Effects on the Civilization of Europe. John Murphy, Baltimore, 1850.
A defense of Catholicism.

Billington, Ray Allen. The Protestant Crusade 1800-1860. Rinehart, New York, 1938 (reissued 1952)
The classic study of anti-Catholicism in early Nineteenth century, with a superior bibliography.

Blanshard, Paul. American Freedom and Catholic Power. Beacon, Boston, 1949 (revised 1958).
Perhaps the most famous polemic in U.S. history, in which author charges that Roman Catholicism is inherently hostile to American concepts of democracy.

Coulton, G. G. Romanism and Truth. Faith Press, London, 1930.
A plea for more honesty in Roman Catholicism's public image.

Curry, Lerond. Protestant-Catholic Relations in America. University of Kentucky, Lexington, 1972.
Brief but adequate survey of tension between conflict and tolerance from 1917 to 1967.

Desmond, Humphrey J. The A.P.A. Movement. New Century Press, Washington, D.C., 1912.
The first book-length treatment of a short lived but powerful anti-Catholic political organization which flourished in the 1890s. Contains letters from A.P.A. founder Henry F. Bowers to author.

Garrett, James Leo. Baptists and Roman Catholicism. Broadman, Nashville, 1965.
A Baptist church-state scholar's short but useful bibliography of Baptist writings on Roman Catholicism. He annotates books of an exposurist, controversial nature.

Garrison, Winfred Ernest. Catholicism and the American Mind. Willett, Clark, and Colby, Chicago, 1928.
Rather critical look at the "mysterious stranger" in American life.

RELIGIOUS CONFLICT

Glock, Charles Y. and Rodney Stark. Religion and Society in Tension.
Rand McNally, Chicago, 1965.
Sociological analysis of religion, politics and social change in
the U.S. and other countries.

Higham, John. Strangers in the Land: Patterns of American Nativism,
1860-1925. Rutgers University, New Brunswick, 1955. Atheneum
Paperback, New York, 1963.
Standard study of religious prejudice.

Kane, John J. Catholic-Protestant Conflicts in America. Regnery,
Chicago, 1955.
A sociologist's attempt to isolate specific areas of misunderstanding.

King, James M. Facing the Twentieth Century. American Union League, New
York, 1899.
A warning to Protestants that their preeminence is fading.

Kinzer, Donald L. An Episode in Anti-Catholicism: The American Protective
Association. University of Washington, Seattle, 1964.
The most complete history of religious conflict in the 1890s.

Laveleye, Emile L. V. Protestantism and Catholicism in their Bearing
Upon the Liberty and Prosperity of Nations. (Introduction by
W. E. Gladstone). Belford, Toronto, 1876.
A strong defense of Protestant culture.

Lee, Robert and Martin E. Marty, eds. Religion and Social Conflict.
Oxford University, New York, 1964.
Notable authorities, including Glock, Roy, Lipset and Herberg,
discuss many aspects of religious group conflict.

Leonard, Ira M. and Robert D. Parmet. American Nativism, 1830-1860.
Van Nostrand, New York, 1971.
Historical survey plus selections from many primary sources.

Lipman, Eugene J. and Albert Vorspan. A Tale of Ten Cities. Union of
American Hebrew Congregations, New York, 1962.
Case studies of religious conflict in such cities as Boston,
Cleveland, Los Angeles, Nashville, New York, Philadelphia, and
St. Paul-Minneapolis. Vivid and sometimes shocking.

Marty, Myron A. Lutherans and Roman Catholicism: The Changing Conflict,
1917-1963. University of Notre Dame, Notre Dame, 1968.
How religious conflict came about and then began to mellow between
two large churches.

Maury, Reuben. The Wars of the Godly; the Story of Religious Conflict in
America. McBride, New York, 1928.
An excellent survey of interfaith conflict.

Moore, John H. Will America Become Catholic? Harper, New York, 1931.
Fair and informative survey, concluding in the negative.

Morgan, Richard E. The Politics of Religious Conflict. Pegasus, New York, 1968.
Sources of church-state tension are depicted and the antagonists viz., the separationists and the accommodationists are identified.

Myers, Gustavus. History of Bigotry in the United States. Random House, New York, 1943. (revised edition Capricorn, New York, 1960).
A classic account of religious prejudice. Highly recommended.

O'Neill, James M. Catholicism and American Freedom. Harper, New York, 1952.
A careful refutation of Paul Blanshard's American Freedom and Catholic Power, though many regard it inferior to Blanshard. Needs to be read in conjunction with Blanshard.

Raab, Earl, ed. Religious Conflict in America. Doubleday, Anchor, New York, 1964.
Stimulating essays by scholars of the caliber of Lenski, Lipset, Herberg, Pelikan, Weigel, Hook, Murray and Pfeiffer on subjects as far-ranging as interfaith marriages, elections and Christmas observances in public schools.

Ray, Mary Augustana. American Opinion of Roman Catholicism in the Eighteenth Century. Columbia University, New York, 1936.
A detailed description of the heritage of anti-Catholicism in Colonial America.

Roussel, Napoleon. Catholic Nations and Protestant Nations, Compared in their Threefold Relation to Wealth, Knowledge and Morality. Ward, London, 1855.
The first systematic attempt to quantify the influence of Catholicism and Protestantism on political, economic and cultural life. Conclusion favorable to Protestantism.

Roy, Ralph Lord. Apostles of Discord. Beacon, Boston, 1953.
An expose of religious bigotry in the early 1950s.

Sanchez, Jose. Anticlericalism: A Brief History. University of Notre Dame, Notre Dame, 1973.
An objective survey of the anti-clerical impulse throughout history, with particular emphasis on Latin Europe.

Schapiro, J. Salwyn. Anticlericalism: Conflict Between Church and State in France, Italy and Spain. Van Nostrand, Princeton, 1967.
Survey of anticlericalism in the three countries where this phenomenon is most manifest. Includes selections from forty four primary source documents.

43

RELIGIOUS CONFLICT

Silcox, Claris Edwin and Galen M. Fisher. Catholics, Jews, and Protestants:
A Study of Relationships in the U.S. and Canada. Harper, New York,
1934.
Reveals a decrease in religious hostility in many areas. Excellent.

Smith, Joseph Jackson. The Impending Conflict between Romanism and
Protestantism in the United States. E. Goodenough, New York, 1871.
The tensions of the era delineated.

Sparrow, William. Romanism and Protestantism Compared as to Their Temporal
Influence. Alexandria, Virginia, 1852.
A short tract defending the Protestants.

Sugrue, Thomas. A Catholic Speaks his Mind on America's Religious Conflict.
Harper, New York, 1952.
A brief but powerfully eloquent ctitique of the materialistic, power-
hungry Roman Catholic hierarchy by a liberal Catholic. Highly controversial when published during the Blanshard-Spellman era.

Williams, Michael. The Shadow of the Pope. Whittlesey House, New York,
1932.
A survey of anti-Catholicism in U.S. history, with special attention
to the Al Smith campaign. Heavily documented.

Winston, Patrick Henry. American Catholics and the A.P.A. Charles H.
Kerr, Chicago, 1895.
A Protestant lawyer defends Catholics from the charge of disloyalty
hurled at them by the A.P.A.

Young, Alfred. Catholic and Protestant Countries Compared in Civilization,
Popular Happiness, General Intelligence, and Morality. Catholic Book
Exchange, New York, 1895.
A defense of Catholic culture.

B. Martyrdom and Persecution.

Arber, Edward, ed. The Torments of Protestant Slaves in the French King's
Galleys, 1686-1707. Elliott Stock, London, 1908.
Despite the flamboyant title, this is considered to be a reasonably
accurate depiction of the persecutions of French Huguenots after the
Revocation of the Edict of Nantes.

Attwater, Donald. Martyrs. Sheed and Ward, New York, 1957.
Lucid sketches of prominent Christian and post-Reformation Roman
Catholic martyrs. Valuable to offset the myth that only Protestants
were persecuted by Rome. Both sides did their share of persecuting
dissenters.

Baird, Henry Martyn. History of the Rise of the Huguenots. 2 volumes.
New York, 1879.
Still a great classic, this treatise admirably portrays the heroic

44

sufferings of the magnificent French Protestants.

Brown, Harold O. J. *The Protest of a Troubled Protestant*. New Rochelle,
New York, 1969.
Contains an excellent chapter "Unanswered Letters to Rome" which
deals with the conservative Protestant's belief that "persecution
has been used as an instrument of policy" by the Roman Church in
the past and may do so again.

Bungener, Laurence. *The Priest and the Huguenot; or, Persecution in the
Age of Louis XV*. Boston, 1854.

Cadoux, C. J. *Roman Catholicism and Freedom*. London, 1936.
A careful evaluation of Rome's historic hostility to religious
liberty with considerable documentation to show that its intolerance
continued in the Twentieth century.

Coulton, G. G. *Inquisition and Liberty*. Beacon, Boston, 1959.
A study of ecclesiastical tyranny and its fear of intellectual freedom.

D'Aubigne, J. H. Merle. *Martyrs of the Reformation*. Presbyterian Board of
Publication, Philadelphia, 1882.
The preeminent French historian's brief martyrology.

Demaus, Robert L. *Hugh Latimer: A Biography*. London, 1903.
A marvelous portrait of the English Bishop of Worcester who was burned
at the stake for refusing to accept the dogma of transubstantiation.

Garrison, W. E. *Intolerance*. Round Table Press, New York, 1934.
A condemnation of religious prejudice wherever found.

Gonsalves, M. J. *Persecutions in Madeira in the Nineteenth Century*. New
York, 1845.
First hand account of anti-Protestant persecution in Portuguese Madeira.

Gray, Tony. *Psalms and Slaughter - A Study in Bigotry*. Heinemann, London,
1972.
Dramatic history of religious prejudice. Intriguing title comes from
old poem about Oliver Cromwell's massacres.

Hauben, Paul, ed. *The Spanish Inquisition*. John Wiley, New York, 1970.
Documentary history in the "Major Issues in History" series.

Horsch, John. *Mennonites in Europe*. Herald Press, Scottdale, Pennsylvania,
1942.
Absorbing history of a persecuted religious minority.

Jurjevic, M. *USTASHA Under the Southern Cross*. Protestant Information
Centre, Melbourne, 1973.
A Croatian Catholic denounces the terrorist activities of his co-
religionists in Australia and traces the anti-Orthodox prejudice
back to the 1940-41 massacre in Croatia.

45

Kalley, Robert R. <u>Persecutions in Madeira in the Nineteenth Century</u>. New York, 1845.
Similar to Gonsalves.

Kimball, Harry. <u>Preach Love, Practice Hate</u>. Masda Publishing Company, 31 Milk Street, Boston, Massachusetts 02109.
Though not well written or scholarly, this book angrily depicts centuries of Christian persecution of the Jewish people.

Lea, Henry Charles. <u>A History of the Inquisition in the Middle Ages</u>. 3 volumes. Russell and Russell, New York, 1955 (reprint of 1888 edition).
Lea was one of the most careful, objective, and truly honest historians whose findings are devastating. Highly recommended.

Loane, Marcus Lawrence. <u>Masters of the English Reformation</u>. London, 1956.
The Anglican Archbishop of Sydney, Australia here presents thumbnail biographical sketches of Thomas Bilney, William Tyndale, Hugh Latimer, Nicholas Ridley and Thomas Cranmer - all marytrs to the Reformed Faith.

Loane, Marcus Lawrence. <u>Pioneers of the Reformation in England</u>. London, 1964.
The leading exponent of Anglican Evangelical values presents sketches of four virtually unknown pioneers of the English Reformation whose lives were snuffed out by the ecclesiastical establishment.

Manhattan, Avro. <u>Catholic Terror Today</u>. Paravision, London, 1970.
Primarily a study of Croatia in 1940-41, with some mention of Spain, Colombia and Northern Ireland.

<u>Martyrdom of the Serbs</u>. Serbian Orthodox Church in the U.S., Chicago, 1943.
Documented eyewitness accounts of the atrocities in Croatia 1940-41.

Montano, Walter. <u>Behind the Purple Curtain</u>. Cowman, Los Angeles, 1950.
A former monk from Peru depicts anti-Protestant violence in Latin America during the 1930s and 1940s.

Norton, Herman. <u>Record of Facts Concerning the Persecutions at Madeira in 1843 and 1846: The Flight of a Thousand Converts to the West Indies and also the Sufferings of Those who Arrived Safely in the United States</u>. New York, 1846.

Norwood, Frederick A. <u>Strangers and Exiles: A History of Religious Refugees</u>. Abingdon, Nashville, 1969.
A masterful two-volume history of religious persecution and exile.

Paisley, Ian. <u>The St. Bartholomew's Day Massacre</u>. Martyrs Memorial Publications, 356 Ravenhill Road, Belfast, 1972.

Ulster's fiery Protestant advocate presents a readable account on the quadricentennial of that awful event.

Paris, Edmond. Genocide in Satellite Croatia. American Institute of Balkan Affairs, Chicago, 1953.
An American but documented account of barbaric religious massacres on an unparalleled scale in Fascist Croatia.

Plaidy, Gene. The Spanish Inquisition: Its Rise, Growth and End. New York, 1967.
An excellent recent survey of the Spanish horrors.

Porteous, David. Calendar of the Reformation. Loizeaux Brothers, New York, 1960. (available from The Convert, P.O. Box 90, Clairton, Pennsylvania, 15025).
A day-by-day account of religious martyrdom in the Reformation and Counter-Reformation Era.

Rand, Philip H. Faithful Unto Death: The Martyrs of East Anglia. Protestant Truth Society, London, 1964.
An emotional but gripping account of persecution of Protestants under Queen Mary in Sixteenth Century England.

Schaff, David Schley. John Huss. New York, 1915.
On the five hundreth anniversary of the burning of the great Bohemian Reformer at the stake, historian Schaff brought out this carefully documented tribute to the life and times of a courageous reformer.

Shelley, Bruce L. The Cross and Flame. Grand Rapids, 1967.
Has been called "a valuable supplement" to Fox's Book of Martyrs, this work treats the history of martyrdom with special reference to the role of the Papacy.

Shobere, Frederic. Persecutions of Popery: Historical Narratives of the Most Remarkable Persecutions Occasioned by the Intolerance of the Church of Rome. New York, 1844.

Smithson, Robert J. The Anabaptists. James Clarke, London, 1935.
Narrative of religious dissenters persecuted by both Protestants and Catholics.

Stephens, R. M. The Burning Bush. London, n.d. Never Failing Light. London, n.d. Both available from Protestant Alliance, 112 Colin Gardens, London, NW9 6ER.
A contemporary Englishman's encounter with the Waldensian Protestants and an appreciation of their struggle for religious freedom.

Strayer, Joseph Reese. The Albigensian Crusades. New York, 1971
A valuable and insightful account of the cruel persecutions of the Albigensians in Southern France.

RELIGIOUS CONFLICT

Sumrall, Lester. Roman Catholicism Slays. Zondervan, Grand Rapids, 1940. Through Fire and Blood in Latin America. Zondervan, Grand Rapids, 1944.
Anti-Protestant persecution vividly depicted.

Turberville, Arthur Stanley. Medieval Heresy and the Inquisition. Archon Books, Hamden, Connecticut, 1964.
Shows the connection between Medieval church corruption and intolerance toward dissenters.

Waagenaar, Sam. The Pope's Jews. Open Court, LaSalle, Illinois, 1974. An internationally acclaimed history of Papal support for anti-Semitism through fifteen centuries. Brilliant, scholarly and definitive.

Wenger, John Christian. Even Unto Death. John Knox, Richmond, 1961. An important and moving account of the heroism and martyrdom of the Sixteenth century Anabaptists in Central Europe.

White, Henry. Massacre of St. Bartholomew. John Murray, London, 1868. Excellent history.

Wilder, John B. The Shadow of Rome. Zondervan, Grand Rapids, 1960. A short survey of religious persecution from the Middle Ages to Colombia and Spain, 1960.

Cross Reference: See section on England in Chapter II.

Chapter V

RELIGION AND POLITICS

In this chapter we will consider the many areas in which religion has affected politics. Our understanding of the term politics will be primarily in the American sense of legislation and elections. Thus, books in this chapter will be concerned with the effect of religion on public policy, both domestic and foreign, and the voting behavior of major American religious groups. There will also be a number of books which treat the subject of religion and the American presidency and investigate the religious views of our 38 presidents.

Adams, James L. The Growing Church Lobby in Washington. Eerdmans, Grand
Rapids, 1970.
The most recent assessment of church lobbying effectiveness in Congress.

Alley, Robert S. So Help Me God: Religion and the Presidency, Wilson to
Nixon. John Knox, Richmond, 1972.
An original investigation into the three types of civil religion
employed by U.S. Presidents, with particular emphasis on recent
occupants of the Presidency.

Barnes, Roswell P. Under Orders: The Churches and Public Affairs. Doubleday,
Garden City, 1961.
The various social and political concerns of America's churches bared.

Barrett, Patricia. Religious Liberty and the American Presidency.
Herder and Herder, New York, 1963.
The definitive account of anti-Catholicism in the 1960 election.
Contains an appendix, pp. 60-148, of the enormous amount of vile
bigotry published in the nether world of American society in a last
ditch attempt to defeat Senator Kennedy. Also includes policy
statements adopted by various groups during the campaign and the text
of Kennedy's address to the Greater Houston Ministerial Association,
September 12, 1960.

Barton, William E. The Soul of Abraham Lincoln. George H. Doran, New
York, 1920.
Lincoln's moral and ethical vision considered.

Blanshard, Paul. God and Man in Washington. Beacon, Boston, 1960.
The church-state battle front as seen by the dean of American
controversy.

Blum, Virgil C. Catholic Parents, Political Eunuchs. North Star Press,
St. Cloud, Minnesota, 1972.
A hard-hitting demand that Catholics unite as an activist political
group to demand certain rights and overthrow "Supreme Court-established
secularism as the religion of the nation". Introduction by Congressman
James J. Delaney of New York.

Bodo, John R. The Protestant Clergy and Public Issues, 1812-1848.
Princeton University, Princeton, 1954.

Bares the far-ranging political activities of the clergy at a time
when their power was growing substantially.

Boller, Paul F. George Washington and Religion. Southern Methodist,
Dallas, 1963.
Our first President's contributions to religious liberty and religious
tolerance analyzed.

Burner, David. The Politics of Provincialism. Alfred A. Knopf, New York,
1968.
Shows how the Democratic party moved from a predominantly rural
Protestant-based party before 1918 to a Catholic urban one, largely
as a result of the "Brown Derby" campaign of Al Smith.

Bonnell, John Sutherland. Presidential Profiles: Religion in the Life of
American Presidents. Westminster, Philadelphia, 1971.
Very sketchy, popularized account of the subject, acceptable for
beginners. Author strangely excludes the two Adams from the
Unitarian category and seems inclined to downgrade the Episcopalian
contingent.

Carlson, John Roy. Under Cover. E. P. Dutton, New York, 1943.
A critique of Father Coughlin's brand of clerical fascism by an anti-
Fascist undercover agent.

Clouse, G. Robert, et. al.,eds. The Cross and the Flag. Creation House,
Carol Stream, Illinois, 1972.
Several evangelical Protestants challenge their community to eschew
"enslavement" to the political right.

Cousins, Norman. In God We Trust: The Religious Beliefs and Ideas of
the American Founding Fathers. Harper, New York, 1958.
Refreshing inquiry.

Coxe, A. Cleveland. The Jesuit Party in American Politics. Boston, 1894.
An Episcopal bishop's unfavorable look at alleged Jesuit political
influence.

Cross, Arthur Lyon. The Anglican Episcopate and the American Colonies.
Longmans Green, New York, 1902. (reprint Archon, Hamden, Connecticut,
1964).
Charges that fear of an Anglican episcopate in the colonies caused
many dissenting Protestants to support the Revolution.

Davis, Lawrence B. Immigrants, Baptists and the Protestant Mind in
America. University of Illinois, Urbana, 1973.
Reveals the changing attitudes of American Protestants toward federal
immigration laws from 1880 to 1925. Author believes Protestants
feared liberal immigration policies were being used as an instrument
of political policy by the Roman Catholic Church to achieve cultural
dominance in the U.S.

RELIGION AND POLITICS

Dawidowicz, Lucy S. and Leon J. Goldstein. <u>Politics in a Pluralist Democracy</u>. Institute of Human Relations Press, New York, 1963.
An important study of Catholic and Jewish voting in the 1960 elections, concluding, interestingly, that Jewish support for Kennedy exceeded the Catholic.

De Leon, Daniel. <u>Ultramontanism; Roman Catholic Political Machine in Action</u>. New York Labor News Company, New York, 1928. (1948 edition called <u>The Vatican in Politics</u>).
A socialist critique of political Catholicism.

Doerr, Edd. <u>The Conspiracy That Failed</u>. Americans United, Washington, D.C., 1968.
An exciting narrative of the unsuccessful attempts to change the Constitution of New York State in 1966-67 to allow state funds for parochial schools.

Dohen, Dorothy Marie. <u>Nationalism and American Catholicism</u>. Sheed and Ward, New York, 1967.
Interesting contention that U.S. Catholicism, in an excessive but understandable desire to become popular, has tended toward excessive patriotism and acceptance of the status quo.

Dulce, Berton and Edward J. Richter. <u>Religion and the Presidency</u>. Macmillan, New York, 1962.
Entertaining, well-documented history of religious issues in Presidential elections from the earliest days of the Republic. About half the book deals with the Kennedy victory in 1960.

Ebersole, Luke E. <u>Church Lobbying in the Nation's Capitol</u>. Macmillan, New York, 1951.
A thorough description of the various church lobbies in Washington at the end of the Truman years.

Feiertag, Sister Loretta Clare. <u>American Public Opinion on the Diplomatic Relations between the United States and the Papal States, 1847-1867</u>. Catholic University of America, Washington, D. C., 1933.
The definitive account of a little known event.

Felknor, Bruce. <u>Dirty Politics</u>. Norton, New York, 1966.
The executive director of the Fair Campaign Practices Committee reviews political and religious smear campaigns in American history.

Fellowship Forum. <u>Proof of Rome's Political Meddling in America</u>. Washington, D. C., 1927.
Alleged expose of the National Catholic Welfare Conference.

Fenton, John. <u>The Catholic Vote</u>. Hauser, New Orleans, 1960.
This is the only full-length study of Catholic voting behavior ever published. Written by a former director of the Gallup Poll, it is a fascinating document, containing much statistical data as well as insightful interpretation.

RELIGION AND POLITICS

Flynn, George Q. American Catholics and the Roosevelt Presidency, 1932-1936. University of Kentucky, Lexington, 1968.
Immensely informed narrative of changing Catholic opinion during FDR's first term and the defection of many Catholic voters during the 1936 election.

Frazier, Claude A., comp. Religion and Politics Can Mix. Broadman, Nashville, 1974.
A collection of rather pious essays by Senators and Governors on the importance of personal religion in public life.

Fuchs, Lawrence. John F. Kennedy and American Catholicism. Meredith, New York, 1967.
A study of Kennedy in the context of the historical development of American Catholicism and as a symbol of a changing, more pluralistic nation.

Fuchs, Lawrence. The Political Behavior of American Jews. Free Press, Glencoe, Illinois, 1956.
A political scientist's scholarly analysis of Jewish voting preferences since Jeffersonian days, with special reference to the 1952 election.

Fuller, Edmund and David E. Green. God in the White House: The Faiths of American Presidents. Crown, New York, 1968.
The best analysis of the theological upbringing and religious sentiments of our Presidents from Washington to Johnson. Includes a brief assessment of each President's religiosity.

Fulton, Justin Dewey. Rome in America. Funk and Wagnalls, New York, 1887.
Castigates Roman Catholic political influence.

Fulton, Justin Dewey. Washington in the Lap of Rome. W. Kellaway, Boston, 1888.
The famous Baptist pastor of Boston's Tremont Temple and ardent anti-Papal critic criticizes growing Roman influence on U.S. politics.

Gurian, Waldemar and M. A. Fitzsimmons, eds. The Catholic Church in World Affairs. University of Notre Dame Press, Notre Dame, 1954.
A superb collection of analyses by leading authorities of the church's important political influence in the major nations of the world, at international deliberations and at the United Nations.

Geyer, Alan Francis. Piety and Politics: American Protestantism in the World Arena. John Knox, Richmond, 1963.
Solid account of Protestant influences on U.S. foreign policy since the Spanish-American War.

Hampton, Vernon B. The Religious Background of the White House. Christopher New York, 1932.
Satisfactory survey.

52

RELIGION AND POLITICS

Hampton, William Judson. The Religion of the Presidents. Somerville,
New Jersey, 1925.
Concise essays on Presidential religion from Washington to Coolidge.

Hefley, James C. and Edward E. Plowman. Washington: Christians in the
Corridors of Power. Tyndale House, Wheaton, 1975. Coverdale House,
London, 1975.
An informative study of the renaissance of evangelical Christianity
in the nation's Capitol, including an interesting chapter on the
religion of President Gerald Ford.

Henderson, Charles P. The Nixon Theology. Harper, New York, 1972.
A Princeton theologian critically examines the rather shallow
theology of the 37th President.

Hero, Alfred O. American Religious Groups View Foreign Policy. Duke
University, Durham, 1973.
A definitive study of Protestant, Catholic, and Jewish public opinion
on major domestic and foreign policy issues from 1937 to 1969.
Includes 275 pages of tables and charts.

High, Stanley. The Church in Politics. New York, 1930.
A summary of the political involvement of the churches, especially
the late Prohibition Campaign which marked the high water of
Protestant power.

Hughey, George Washington. Political Romanism. Carlton and Lanahan,
New York and Cincinnati, 1872.
A refutation of the belief that Catholicism is compatible with
democracy.

Humphrey, Edward F. Nationalism and Religion in America, 1774-1789.
Chipman, Boston, 1924.
A survey of religious influences on the American Revolution, showing
how and why the various religious groups lined up as they did.

Hyland, James A. Rome and the White House. Devin-Adair, New York, 1928.
Defends the Catholic Church against the charge that an Al Smith
victory would lead to Papal control of the U.S. government.

Isaacs, Stephen D. Jews and American Politics. Doubleday, New York, 1974.
The best account of Jewish involvement in U.S. politics by a journalist
whose volume also includes a good bibliography and a list of all Jewish
Governors, Senators and Congressmen in American history.

Isely, Bliss. Presidents, Men of Faith. Wilde, Boston, 1953.
Insightful investigation of Presidential religion from Washington
to Truman.

Jamieson, William F. The Clergy, a Source of Danger to the American Republic.
Chicago, 1873.
A polemic against political meddling by preachers.

Kenney, David, et. al. Roll Call! Patterns of Voting in the Sixth
    Illinois Constitutional Convention. University of Illinois Press,
    Urbana, 1975.
    An imaginative analysis of factors which influence the voting
    behavior of delegates to a Constitutional revision convention.
    Contains an important discussion of denominational voting patterns
    and religious-ethical issues like parochial school aid, abortion,
    and public school prayer.

Kersten, Lawrence L. The Lutheran Ethic. Wayne State University, Detroit,
    1970.
    Contains valuable information on Lutheran voting behavior and
    political views held by American Lutherans.

Kinsman, Frederick J. Americanism and Catholicism. Longmans-Green,
    New York, 1924.
    The former Episcopal Bishop of Delaware, a recent Roman Catholic
    convert, defends the Roman Church from the charge that it is hostile
    and antithetical to democracy and church-state separation.

LaNoue, George R. Bibliography of Doctoral Dissertations Undertaken in
    American and Canadian Universities, 1940-1962, on Religion and
    Politics. New York, 1963.

Lansing, Isaac J. Romanism and the Republic. Arnold, Boston, 1890.
    An early Paul Blanshard-like critique of authoritarian clericalism
    in the political arena.

Lenski, Gerhard Emmanuel. The Religious Factor. Doubleday, Garden City,
    1961.
    A classic sociological study of how religion makes an impact on
    political and economic life.

Levy, Mark R. and Michael S. Kramer. The Ethnic Factor: How America's
    Minorities Decide Elections. Simon and Schuster, New York, 1972.
    (revised 1973 edition).
    Two political journalists analyze the important influence on
    elections wielded by Jews and many Catholic ethnic groups.
    Essential reading.

Lewy, Guenther. Religion and Revolution. Oxford University Press, New
    York, 1973.
    Far-ranging essays on the correlative relationships between religious
    groups and revolutionary movements. The chapter on the Catholic
    Church and the Spanish Civil War is exceptionally useful.

Maier, Hans. Revolution and Church: The Early History of Christian
    Democracy, 1789-1901. University of Notre Dame, Notre Dame, 1969.
    A scholarly philosophical study of political Catholicism.

Manhattan, Avro. Catholic Power Today. Lyle Stuart, New York, 1967.
    A critical study of Catholic political influence throughout the world.

RELIGION AND POLITICS

Marshall, Charles C. Governor Smith's American Catholicism. Dodd Mead, New York, 1928.
A concise critique of Al Smith's contention that he would not be unduly influenced by church officials if he were President.

Mecklenburg, George. Bowing the Preacher Out of Politics. Revell, New York, 1928.
Demands that churches and preachers "strike out with righteous indignation" against the evils of society. Helps to explain why so many Protestant clergy were intimately involved in politics, especially during the Prohibition campaign.

Metzger, Charles H. Catholics and the American Revolution: A Study in Religious Climate. Loyola University Press, Chicago, 1962.
Catholic influences on the Revolutionary era considered.

Michener, James A. Report of the County Chairman. Random House, New York, 1961.
The famed author was a campaign coordinator for Senator John F. Kennedy in 1960 and reveals the "flood" of anti-Catholicism in Bucks County Pennsylvania during the Fall of 1960.

Miller, John Chester. Origins of the American Revolution. Little Brown, Boston, 1943.
Shows how religious conflicts were causes of the War for Independence.

Miller, William Lee. Piety Along the Potomac. Houghton Mifflin, Boston, 1964.
A delightfully sardonic look at the manipulative use of religion for political ends during the Eisenhower years.

Miller, William Lee. The Protestant and Politics. Westminster, Philadelphia, 1965.
Urges citizen involvement to insure ethical ideals are manifest.

Moore, Edmund A. A Catholic Runs for President. Ronald, New York, 1956.
A dramatic and vivid account of the Al Smith campaign and the lurid anti-Catholicism which erupted.

Morton, Elizabeth. Rome and Washington. Jones, Chicago, 1899.
Unfavorable consideration of Roman Catholic influence on U.S. politics.

Morton, Frances T. The Roman Catholic Church and its Relation to the Federal Government. R. G. Badger, Boston, 1909.
Unsympathetic tone.

Nations, Gilbert O. The Political Career of Alfred E. Smith. The Protestant, Washington, D. C., 1928.
A savage attack on the New York Governor, finding him ineligible for the Presidency because of his religion.

Nations, Gilbert O. <u>Rome in Congress</u>. The Protestant, Washington, D. C., 1925.
Warns Protestants of increasing Catholic political influence.

Nichols, Roy F. <u>Religion and American Democracy</u>. Louisiana State University, Baton Rouge, 1959.
The correlation and interaction between religion and government.

Odegard, Peter H., ed. <u>Religion and Politics</u>. Oceana, Dobbs Ferry, New York, 1960.
Fascinating essays, particularly on religious prejudice in the political arena.

Overdyke, W. Darrell. <u>The Know-Nothing Party in the South</u>. Louisiana State University, Baton Rouge, 1950.
Scholarly history.

Peel, Roy Victor and Thomas C. Donnelly. <u>The 1928 Campaign, an Analysis</u>. R. R. Smith, New York, 1931 (reprint Arno, New York, 1974).
Two political scientists analyze the effect of anti-Catholicism on the Hoover-Smith election, though most of the book deals with other issues.

Pierard, Richard V. <u>The Unequal Yoke</u>. Lippincott, Philadelphia, 1970.
An evangelical theologian calls for the termination of the alliance between political conservatism and religious conservatism.

Pratt, John Webb. <u>Religion, Politics and Diversity: The Church-State Theme in New York History</u>. Cornell University Press, Ithaca, 1967.
Religion has influenced New York politics for over a century.

Pike, James A. <u>A Roman Catholic in the White House</u>. Doubleday, New York, 1960.
The controversial liberal Episcopal bishop discusses the interfaith tensions and conflicts of the 1950s which made the possible election of a Catholic President so frightening to many Protestants.

Richey, Russell E. and Donald G. Jones, eds. <u>American Civil Religion</u>. Harper, New York, 1974.
Essays on many aspects of the controversy.

Rischin, Moses. <u>Our Own Kind</u>. Center for the Study of Democratic Institutions, Santa Barbara, 1960.
A study of how and why many people vote on religious or ethnic lines, with particular emphasis on the 1956 election.

Ryan, John A. and Francis J. Boland. <u>Catholic Principles of Politics</u>. Macmillan, New York, 1940.
Conservative Catholic exegesis which would be regarded as reactionary today.

RELIGION AND POLITICS

Schauinger, J. Herman. Profiles in Action: American Catholics in
Political Life. Bruce, Milwaukee, 1966.
The only volume ever written about Catholic statesmen and politicians
in U.S. history. Includes signers of the Constitution, legislators,
Supreme Court justices, cabinet officers, senators, congressmen,
governors and one president. Indispensable reading.

Schroeder, Theodore. Al Smith, the Pope and the Presidency. New York
1928.
A rationalist-humanist fears that "political Romanism" would
outweigh Smith's personal progressivism.

Scisco, Louis D. Political Nativism in New York State. New York, 1901.
A historical sketch of the bitter anti-Catholicism in Nineteenth
century New York State politics.

Settel, T. S., ed. The Faith of JFK. Dutton, New York, 1965.
Includes President Kennedy's favorite Bible quotations, inspirational
poetry, and a collection of his public messages dealing with religious
topics. Introduction by Cardinal Cushing.

Silva, Ruth C. Rum, Religion and Votes. Pennsylvania State University,
University Park, Pennsylvania, 1962.
Statistical and analytic study of the Al Smith campaign.

Sperry, Willard L. The Meaning of God in the Life of Lincoln. Central
Church, Boston, 1922.
Lincoln's role as prophet and preacher.

Stedman, Murray S. Religion and Politics in America. Harcourt, Brace
and World, New York, 1964.
A study of religious influence on elections and the development of
public policies, and churches as interest groups.

Steiner, Franklin. Religious Beliefs of our Presidents. New York, 1936.
From Washington to FDR.

Streiker, Lowell D. and Gerald S. Strober. Religion and the New Majority.
Association Press, New York, 1972.
Two liberal Protestant scholars analyze contemporary religious
fundamentalism personified by Billy Graham and relate it to
increasing Middle American political conservatism.

Thomas, W. H. The Roman Catholic in American Politics. Albion, Boston,
1895.
A journalist's portrait of the growing political influence of a
minority.

Trueblood, Elton. Abraham Lincoln: Theologian of American Anguish.
Harper, New York, 1973.
The eminent Quaker theologian's perceptive and compassionate
elucidation of Lincoln's religious, moral and ethical views. An

impressive study.

Weyl, Nathaniel. The Jew in American Politics. Arlington House, New
    Rochelle, 1968.
    An historical survey of Jewish participation in American politics
    by a foremost representative of a rare breed - a Jewish conservative.

Wilson, E. Raymond. Uphill for Peace: Quaker Impact on Congress.
    Friends United Press, Richmond, Indiana, 1975.
    Case study of an effective registered religious lobby.

Wolf, William J. The Almost Chosen People. New York, 1959.
    A study of Abraham Lincoln's almost prophetic moral and ethical
    views.

Wolf, William J. Lincoln's Religion. Pilgrim, Philadelphia, 1970.
    An Episcopal theologian's perceptive analysis, it deals carefully
    with the charges made by Lincoln's law partner William H. Herndon
    that Lincoln was a skeptic and agnostic.

Yinger, J. Milton. Religion and the Struggle for Power. Duke University,
    Durham, North Carolina, 1946.
    Primarily concerned with the activities of organized religion in the
    economic sphere.

Chapter VI

CHURCH, STATE AND EDUCATION

Many church-state conflicts have been settled in the educational arena. Books in this chapter deal with three basic areas. The first will be the question of government financial assistance to church-related or parochial schools, which has been a major political issue in this country since the 1820s. Books treating the nature and scope of parochial education as well as the role of the government in the financing of parochial education will be considered in this first section. The second section considers the question of religion in universities or colleges. The third section includes books on an all-important subject - religion in the public schools. Disputes over prayer and Bible reading as well as the objective study of religion in public schools will be included.

A. Parochial Education

Bartell, Ernest. Costs and Benefits of Catholic Elementary and Secondary Schools. University of Notre Dame, Notre Dame, 1969.
Primarily an economic analysis of parochial schools in the context of all education.

Beach, Fred Francis and Robert F. Will. The State and Nonpublic Schools. U.S. Department of Health, Education, and Welfare, Washington, D.C., 1958.
A handbook of state and federal regulations.

Beck, Walter H. Lutheran Elementary Schools in the U.S. Concordia, St. Louis, 1939.
Brief history.

Benjamin, Marge. Three Out of Ten: The Nonpublic Schools of New York City. New York Department of City Planning, New York, 1972.
A comprehensive overview of the private and parochial schools in the nation's largest city.

Bishop, Claire Huchet. How Catholics Look at Jews. Paulist, New York, 1974.
A critical look at anti-Semitism in Catholic school textbooks in Italy, Spain, France, Switzerland, Belgium and Canada by a French Catholic scholar.

Blum, Virgil C. Catholic Education: Survival or Demise? Argus, Chicago, 1969.
A defense of the necessity of separate Catholic schools, coupled with a plea for government assistance and an attack on alleged WASP domination of the U.S. government and culture.

Blum, Virgil C. Freedom in Education. Doubleday, 1965.
The leading theoretician of government aid to parochial schools maintains that such assistance is desirable and constitutional.

He includes an approving look at countries which do subsidize religious schools.

Blum, Virgil C. Freedom of Choice. Macmillan, New York, 1958, 1960.
A defense of parochiaid. Reissued and revised edition entitled
Freedom of Choice in Education. (Paulist, New York, 1963).

Boffa, Conrad H. Canonical Provisions for Catholic Schools. Catholic
University of America, Washington, D. C., 1939.
An explanation of all the canon law provisions pertaining to
education.

Brekke, Milo. How Different Are People Who Attended Lutheran Schools?
Concordia, St. Louis, 1974.
A socio-educational study of Lutheran parochial schools which
concludes that parochial school students are at least marginally
"better" in a number of measurements, and that they are more likely
to remain loyal, practicing Lutherans. The schools evidently make
a significant difference in the educational and religious formation
of the children.

Brickman, William W. and Stanley Lehrer, eds. Religion, Government and
Education. Society for the Advancement of Education, New York, 1961.
An anthology of germane essays by leading authorities plus a unique
and very helpful chronology of church-state relations in American
education from 1600 to 1961. Also contains a comprehensive look at
religion and the schools throughout the world.

Brown, William E. and Andrew M. Greeley. Can Catholic Schools Survive?
Sheed and Ward, New York, 1970.
Authors expound the view that Catholic schools have a relatively
promising future if the church will commit additional resources to
develop a flexible, modern system of education.

Buetow, Harold A. Of Singular Benefit: The Story of Catholic Education
in the United States. Macmillan, New York, 1970.
A splendid historical study which surpasses all rivals. Heavily
documented.

Burns, James A. and Bernard J. Kohlbrenner. A History of Catholic Education
in the United States. Benziger, New York, 1937. (reprint Arno, New
York, 1969)
Long the standard history, this is a revision of two volumes originally
written by Father Burns and published in 1908 and 1912.

Callahan, Daniel J., ed. Federal Aid and Catholic Schools. Helicon,
Baltimore, 1964.
Ten authorities, both pro and con, express their views on this contro-
versial topic. An appendix summarizes the policies in effect in
Britain, Germany, Canada and Italy.

CHURCH, STATE AND EDUCATION

Carman, Kenneth W. Crusade in Michigan: The Parochiaid Story. Garden
    City, Michigan, 1970 (available from Americans United, Silver Spging,
    Maryland).
    A privately-printed but very detailed history of the battles over
    parochial school aid in the Michigan legislature, including roll
    call votes in both houses.

Cogdell, Gaston. What Price Parochiaid? Americans United, Washington,
    D.C., 1968.
    A weighty statement of the case against government aid to parochial
    schools.

Crowley, Jeremiah. The Parochial School - A Curst to the Church, a
    Menace to the Nation. Chicago, 1905.
    A former priest's jeremiad against parochial education.

Deferrari, Roy J. Complete System of Catholic Education is Necessary.
    Daughters of St. Paul, Boston, 1964.
    A rebuttal to Mary Perkins Ryan's Are Parochial Schools the Answer?
    by one who regards separate education for Catholics as vital.

Deferrari, Roy J., ed. Vital Problems of Catholic Education in the United
    States. Catholic University of America, Washington, D.C., 1939.
    A symposium.

De Hovre, Franz. Catholicism in Education. Benziger, New York, 1934.
    A comparative analysis of the educational views of five famous
    Catholic thinkers including Cardinal Newman and Cardinal Mercier.

Diffley, Jerome E. Catholic Reaction to American Public Education.
    Univeristy of Notre Dame, Notre Dame, 1959.
    Shows the varied but generally critical posture of U.S. Catholics.

Dorchester, Daniel. Romanism Versus the Public School System. Phillips
    and Hunt, New York, 1888.
    A Methodist church statistician and historian criticizes Roman Catholic
    unfriendliness toward public education.

Dunn, James B. The Pope's Last Veto in American Politics. Committee of
    One Hundred, Boston, 1890.
    Protestant-Catholic agitation over the school question occasioned
    this Protestant document.

Dushkin, Alexander M. Jewish Education in New York City. Bureau of Jewish
    Education, New York, 1918.
    The development of Hebrew day schools described.

Duvall, Sylvanus Milne. The Methodist Episcopal Church and Education up to
    1869. Columbia University, New York, 1928.
    Historical study of early Methodism's interest in education.

CHURCH, STATE AND EDUCATION

Eby, Frederick. _Early Protestant Educators_. New York, 1931.
Shows the contribution of Protestantism to education.

Erickson, Donald A., ed. _Public Controls for Nonpublic Schools_. University
of Chicago, Chicago, 1969.
An analysis of desirable and undesirable interplay between public and
private schools, by an admirer of nonpublic education.

Fichter, Joseph H. _Parochial School: A Sociological Study_. University of
Notre Dame, Notre Dame, 1958.
Before the Greeley-Rossi studies, this was the standard socio-
cultural study of Catholic schools and many of its insights and
interpretations are still valid.

_The Fleischmann Report on the Quality, Cost, and Financing of Elementary
and Secondary Education in New York State_. Viking, New York, 1973.
Impartial inquiry, concluding that government aid to parochial
schools is unnecessary and undesirable.

Friedlander, Anna Fay. _The Shared Time Strategy: Prospects and Trends in
the Growing Partnership Between Public and Church Schools_. Concordia,
St. Louis, 1966.
Brief but informative study of the shared time concept with a listing
of major court decisions affecting the issue. Includes a good
bibliography.

Gabel, Richard J. _Public Funds for Church and Private Schools_. Catholic
University of America, Washington, D. C., 1937.
A defense of using public funds for religiously affiliated schools.

Gabert, Glen. _In Hoc Signo?: A Brief History of Catholic Parochial
Education in America_. Kennikat, Port Washington, New York, 1973.
A rather non-technical and selective review of Catholic education by
an educator who sees parochial education declining in esteem by
Catholics themselves. Highly critical of clerical leadership.
Gabert relates the changes in parochial education to the ethnic
group which dominated American Catholicism at the time, a highly
original view.

Gaebelein, Frank E. _Christian Education in a Democracy_. Oxford University,
New York, 1951.
An attempt to resolve the conflict between religious knowledge and
the requirements of neutrality in a democracy's school systems.

Goebel, Edmund J. _A Study of Catholic Secondary Education during the
Colonial Period up to the First Plenary Council of Baltimore_.
Benziger, New York, 1937.
Informative history.

Greeley, Andrew M. and Peter H. Rossi. _The Education of Catholic Americans_.
Aldine, Chicago, 1966. (Doubleday, Anchor, New York, 1968)
A now much-quoted study of values imparted by Catholic schools.

CHURCH, STATE AND EDUCATION

Healey, Robert M. The French Achievement: Private School Aid, a Lesson
for America. Paulist, New York, 1974.
A Presbyterian seminary professor uses the French system of parochial
school aid as a model for America to emulate.

Horne, H. H. The Philosophy of Christian Education. Revell, New York,
1937.
Evangelical viewpoint lucidly expressed.

Hurley, Mark J., ed. The Declaration on Christian Education of Vatican
Council II. Paulist, Glen Rock, New Jersey, 1966.
Shows the permanence of Catholic educational objectives.

Jellison, Helen M., ed. State and Federal Laws Relating to Nonpublic
Schools. U.S. Department of Health, Education and Welfare, Washington,
D.C., 1975.
The most recent study of state constitutional provisions and operative
federal programs on private school aid for each state. Absolutely
essential for researchers.

Kienel, Paul A. The Christian School: Why it is Right for Your Child.
Victor, Wheaton, Illinois, 1974.
A defense of Protestant parochial schooling.

Koob, C. Albert and Russell Shaw. S.O.S. for Catholic Schools. Holt,
Rinehart and Winston, New York, 1970.
An "insiders" appraisal of the financial, pedagogical and functional
problems of parochial education in a time of tension.

Koob, C. Albert, ed. What is Happening to Catholic Education? National
Catholic Educational Association, Washington, D.C., 1966.
A Catholic educator's inside look.

Kraushaar, Otto F. American Nonpublic Schools. Johns Hopkins, Baltimore,
1972.
A highly sympathetic study of private and parochial education by a
prominent educator and professor at the Harvard Graduate School of
Education.

Lannie, Vincent P. Public Money and Parochial Education: Bishop Hughes,
Governor Seward, and the New York School Controversy. Case Western
Reserve University, Cleveland, 1968.
One of the best histories of a crucial event available.

La Noue, George R., ed. Educational Vouchers: Concepts and Controversies.
Teacher's College Press of Columbia University, New York, 1972.
An anthology of essays by both proponents and critics of the
Voucher plan.

Larson, Martin A. When Parochial Schools Close. Robert B. Luce, Inc.,
Washington, D. C., 1972.
A study in educational financing which concentrates on sixteen

communities whose parochial schools either declined grievously or went out of business altogether. Author concludes that the closure of parochial schools and the transfer of many of their pupils to public schools did not adversely affect the tax structure of the community or result in deteriorating public schools.

Lee, James Michael, ed. Catholic Education in the Western World. University of Notre Dame, Notre Dame, 1967. Very informative essays by specialists on Catholic schools and government support in France, Germany, the Netherlands, Italy, England and the United States.

McCluskey, Neil G. Catholic Education Faces its Future. Doubleday, New York, 1969. Sympathetic, positive orientation.

McCluskey, Neil G. Catholic Education in America: A Documentary History. William Byrd Press, Richmond, 1964.

McCluskey, Neil G. Catholic Viewpoint on Education. Doubleday Image, New York, 1962. This is probably still the best rationale for a separate Catholic school system available, by a leading authority who is now dean of the department of education at Herbert Lehman College in New York.

McGucken, William. The Jesuits and Education. Bruce, Milwaukee, 1932. History cum justification.

McGucken, William. The Catholic Way in Education. Bruce, Milwaukee, 1934. A systematic exposition of the position that religious values must be primary in all education.

McLaughlin, Sr. Raymond. A History of State Legislation Affecting Private Elementary and Secondary Schools in the United States, 1870-1945. Catholic University of America, Washington, D. C., 1946.

McLoughlin, Emmet. American Culture and Catholic Schools. Lyle Stuart, New York, 1960. A devastatingly critical analysis. Author contends Catholic education is inferior indoctrination.

Mary Janet, Sister. Catholic Secondary Education: A National Survey. Catholic University of America, Washington, D.C., 1949.

Neuwien, Reginald A., ed. Catholic Schools in Action. University of Notre Dame, Notre Dame and London, 1966. Results of a sociological survey on the attitudes of students, parents, and staff to the goals of Catholic education.

O'Brien, Kevin J. The Proximate Aim of Education. Bruce, Milwaukee, 1958. Classical scholasticism defended in a penetrating philosophical tract.

CHURCH, STATE AND EDUCATION

O'Connell, Laurence John. Are Catholic Schools Progressive? B. Herder,
     St. Louis, 1946.
     An affirmative conclusion.

Office for Educational Research, University of Notre Dame. Economic
     Problems of Nonpublic Schools. Notre Dame, Indiana, 1971.
     An economic analysis prepared for President Nixon's Commission on
     School Finance. Massive and detailed.

Pawlikowski, John T. Catechetics and Prejudice. Paulist, New York, 1973.
     A provocative analysis of Catholic school textbooks, revealing
     widespread anti-Jewish and anti-Protestant biases. Author is a
     Catholic priest who urges major changes in textbook writing.

Phelan, Jeremiah. Which are the More Godless, the Public or Parochial
     Schools? Rochester, New York, 1917.
     Provocative and controversial.

Powell, Theodore. The School Bus Law. Wesleyan University, Middletown,
     Connecticut, 1960.
     Analysis of busing as a method of helping parochial schools.

Redden, John D. and Francis A. Ryan. A Catholic Philosophy of Education.
     Bruce, Milwaukee, 1956.
     A conservative Catholic view originally designed as a college text.

Reilly, Daniel F. The School Controversy, 1891-1893. Catholic University
     of America, Washington, D.C., 1943.
     Standard, documented history.

Richardson, N. E. The Christ of the Classroom. Macmillan, New York, 1931.
     How religion may challenge and enrich students.

Ryan, Mary Perkins. Are Parochial Schools the Answer? Holt, Rinehart and
     Winston, New York, 1964.
     One of the most controversial books in this field, the author contends
     that parochial schools have outlived their usefulness and have become
     an obstacle to a truly Christian, ecumenical education.

Ryan, Mary Perkins. We're All in this Together: Issues and Options in the
     Education of Catholics. Holt, Rinehart and Winston, New York, 1972.
     Updating of her earlier book, expressing more conservative views.

Schisler, John Q. Christian Teaching in the Churches. Abingdon, Nashville,
     1954.
     A conservative Protestant plea for teaching about God and the Bible
     in public schools.

Shaw, Russell B., ed. Trends and Issues in Catholic Education. Citation,
     New York, 1969.
     Collection of articles on contemporary problems faced by a declining
     school system.

CHURCH, STATE AND EDUCATION

Sherrill, Lewis Joseph. Presbyterian Parochial Schools. Yale University
Press, New Haven, 1932.
The only full-length study available.

Shuster, George N. Catholic Education in a Changing World. Holt, Rinehart
and Winston, New York, 1968.
Wise and insightful viewpoint.

Smith Sherman M. The Relation of the State to Religious Education in
Massachusetts. Syracuse, 1934.
Updating of 1926 book.

Smith, Sherman M. Religious Education in Massachusetts. Syracuse, 1926.
History of religious influences on state schools.

Spalding, John L. Education and the Future of Religion. Ave Maria, Notre
Dame, Indiana, 1901.
A famous Archbishop's statement.

Sullivan, Daniel J. Public Aid to Nonpublic Schools. D. C. Heath,
Lexington, Massachusetts, 1974.
An economist's survey, concluding that public aid is not desirable
or economically feasible.

Tax Credits for Nonpublic Education. Hearings before the Committee on Ways
and Means, House of Representatives, Ninety Second Congress. 3 volumes.
U.S. Government Printing Office, Washington, D.C., 1972.

U.S. Office of Education. Dual Enrollment in Public and Non-Public Schools.
U.S. Government Printing Office, Washington, D.C., 1965.
Nationwide survey results.

Ward, Leo R. New Life in Catholic Schools. Herder and Herder, New York,
1958.
Author challenges parochial school administrators to place more emphasis
on scholarship, academics, and freedom of inquiry in the curriculum.

B. Religion and Higher Education

Allen, Henry E., ed. Religion in the State University. Burgess,
Minneapolis, 1950.
Legal limitations, recent trends and special problems are considered
by state university administrators and faculty in Minnesota.

Bach, Marcus. Of Faith and Learning: The Story of the School of Religion
at the State University of Iowa. University of Iowa, Iowa City, 1952.
A popular description of the famous school of religion regarded by
many as a pioneer in the field.

Boyer, Edward Sterling. Religion in the American College. New York, 1930.
The importance of maintaining courses in religion argued.

CHURCH, STATE AND EDUCATION

Brown, Kenneth I. Not Minds Alone. Harper, New York, 1954.
A plea for restoration of ethical and spiritual values as preeminent
in a college community.

Butler, Richard. God on the Secular Campus. Doubleday, New York, 1963.
A Newman chaplain describes the whole panorama of interaction between
religion and the secular groves of academe. Critical of alleged
iconoclasm and humanistic penetration of secular institutes of
higher learning.

Cuninggim, Merrimon. The College Seeks Religion. Yale University Press,
New Haven, 1947.
An historical-practical survey which concludes that more interest in
religion in an objective context is the trend since World War I.
Compares the type of programs available in public, private and church-
related colleges.

Earnshaw, George L., et. al., eds. The Campus Ministry. Judson, Valley
Forge, 1964.
A concise history of "Student Christian Movements" since the 1690s.

Espy, R. H. The Religion of College Teachers: The Beliefs, Practices
and Religious Preparation of Faculty Members in Church-Related Colleges.
Association Press, New York, 1951.
An interesting and virtually unique analysis of the theological
orientation of Protestant college instructors.

Fairchild, Hoxie N., ed. Religious Perspectives in College Teaching.
Ronald, New York, 1952.
A treatment of the ways in which religion can affect various secular
disciplines, including music, history, literature, economics, and
science.

Gauss, Christian F., ed. The Teaching of Religion in American Higher
Education. Ronald Press, New York, 1951.
A symposium of prominent educators attempts to establish viable
guidelines for a complex question.

Gelhorn, Walter and R. Kent Greenawalt. The Sectarian College and the
Public Purse. Oceana, Dobbs Ferry, 1970.
Two attorneys reveal how they charted the secularization of Fordham
University in order to secure public funds for the one-time Jesuit
college.

Godbold, Albea. The Church College of the Old South. Duke University,
Durham, 1944.
Shows deep religiosity in early higher education.

Greeley, Andrew M. The Changing Catholic College. Aldine, Chicago, 1967.
Socio-cultural look at institutions undergoing rapid change.

CHURCH, STATE AND EDUCATION

Hassenger, Robert, ed. _The Shape of Catholic Higher Education_. University of Chicago, Chicago, 1967.
Essays by many authorities.

Hintz, Howard William. _Religion and Public Higher Education_. Brooklyn College, Brooklyn, 1955.
Good general introduction.

Hoge, Dean R. _Commitment on Campus: Changes in Religion and Values Over Five Decades_. Westminster, Philadelphia, 1974.
A unique study of available research material from a dozen colleges, showing massive changes in religious outlook since the 1920s.

Holmes, Arthur F. _The Idea of a Christian College_. Eerdmans, Grand Rapids, 1974.
An attempt to define a Christian college as a synthesizer of human and spiritual values, imparting a unique worldview to its students.

Houston, William. _The Church at the University_. Colombus, Ohio, 1926.
A look at the college chaplaincy programs.

Hutchins, Robert Maynard. _Morals, Religion, and Higher Education_. University of Chicago Press, Chicago, 1950.
A plea for more emphasis on morality and ethics in American colleges.

Lawler, Justus G. _The Catholic Dimension in Higher Education_. Newman, Westminster, 1959.
A thoughtful reflection on the unique purposes and values of religiousl oriented colleges.

Limpert, Paul M., ed. _College Teaching and Christian Values_. Association Press, New York, 1951.
Specialists in eight secular fields discuss the possibility of Christian permeation in the context of church-related colleges.

McCoy, Charles S. _The Responsible Campus: Toward a New Identity for the Church-Related College_. United Methodist Board of Education, Nashville, 1972.
Calls for a redirection of values and a reordering of priorities for church colleges.

Michaelsen, Robert. _The Study of Religion in American Universities_. Society for Religion in Higher Education, New Haven, 1965.
Excellent survey of ten universities.

Pattillo, Manning M. and Donald M. MacKenzie. _Church-Sponsored Higher Education in the United States_. American Council on Education, Washington, D.C., 1966.
A sympathetic portrait of church colleges and their contribution to American culture.

CHURCH, STATE AND EDUCATION

Patton, Leslie Karr. The Purposes of Church-Related Colleges. New York, 1940.
Reasoned statement of the raison d'etre.

Porter, David Richard, ed. The Church in the Universities. New York, 1925.
How religious groups care for the religious welfare of their adherents in secular colleges.

Power, Edward J. A History of Catholic Higher Education in the United States. Bruce, Milwaukee, 1958.
Still the most comprehensive treatment of a relatively unknown field.

Reinert, Paul C. The Urban Catholic University. Sheed and Ward, New York, 1970.
The President of St. Louis University offers his justification for the existence of Catholic universities and the positive role they can play in urban America.

Schuster, George N. Education and Moral Wisdom. Harper, New York, 1960.
Prominent Catholic educator and one-time President of Hunter College urges universities to educate students toward the pursuit of truth and wisdom.

Scimecca, Joseph and Roland Damiano. Crisis at St. Johns: Strike and Revolution on the Catholic Campus. Random House, New York, 1967.
Two faculty members who were intimately involved with the legendary strike at St. Johns University in 1966 present their case plus a demand for modernization and enhanced respect for academic freedom in Catholic colleges.

Searles, Herbert Leon. The Study of Religion in State Universities. University of Iowa, Iowa City, 1927.
A well-documented survey of the subject during the Jazz Age.

Shedd, Clarence Prouty. The Church Follows Its Students. Yale University, New Haven, 1938.
An early history of church chaplaincies on secular campuses.

Smith, Seymour A. The American College Chaplaincy. New York, 1954.
The most complete history of the chaplaincy movement at secular colleges.

Wakin, Edward. The Catholic Campus. Macmillan, New York, 1963.
An assessment of the uniqueness of Catholic colleges plus portraits of the socio-cultural style of eight representative colleges.

Walter, Erich A. Religion and the State University. University of Michigan, Ann Arbor, 1958.
Philosophy, objectives and practical implementation considered.

Ward, Leo R. Blueprint for a Catholic University. Herder and Herder, New York, 1949.
Primarily an historical study rather than a rationale for a distinctly

69

Catholic college.

C. Religion in Public Schools

Adams, Marjorie E., ed. God in the Classroom. National Educators
    Fellowship, South Pasadena, California, 1970.
    A conservative look at the place of religion in the school.

American Association of School Administrators. Religion in the Public
    Schools. Harper, New York, 1964.
    Succinct survey of what should and should not be done.

American Council on Education. The Function of the Public Schools in
    Dealing with Religion. Washington, D.C., 1953.
    The third of a series of reports on the role of religion in the
    public school curriculum. Includes results of a questionnaire sent
    to prominent educators, clergymen, and community leaders. Includes
    valuable bibliography of periodical articles, dissertations, agreed
    syllabuses of religious instruction and mimeographed reports of
    local and state programs.

American Council on Education. The Relation of Religion to Public
    Education. Washington, D.C., 1947.
    Report of a study committee to determine how religion can be
    included in the curriculum in face of increasing secularization.

American Council on Education. Religion and Public Education. Washington,
    D.C., 1944.
    A summary of the principal addresses and discussions at a conference
    of educators, held at Princeton, New Jersey May 12-14, 1944.

Barker, Ernest. Church, State and Education. University of Michigan,
    Ann Arbor, 1957.
    Nine philosophical essays originally published by Methuen and
    Company, London, 1930. Essay on "A Huguenot Theory of Politics"
    is especially rewarding.

Bedsole, Adolph. The Supreme Court Decision on Bible Reading and Prayer;
    America's Black Letter Day. Baker, Grand Rapids, 1964.
    A Fundamentalist Protestant tirade.

Beggs, David W., ed. America's Schools and Churches; Partners in Conflict.
    Indiana University, Bloomington, 1966.
    Interesting essays expressing diverse viewpoints.

Bell, Sadie. The Church, the State and Education in Virginia. Science
    Press, Philadelphia, 1930. (reprint Arno Press, New York, 1969).
    Massive (796 page) study.

Beman, Lamar Taney. Religious Teaching in the Public Schools. H.W. Wilson,
    New York, 1927.

70

CHURCH, STATE AND EDUCATION

A state-by-state survey of laws regulating religious teaching in public schools.

Bernstein, Diana and Iva Cohen. Church, State and Education; a Selected Bibliography. American Jewish Committee, New York, 1949.

The Bible in the Public Schools. Robert Clarke and Company, Cincinnati, 187 1870. (reprint by Da Capo Press, New York, 1967).
Opinions of the Cincinnati Superior Court, plus interested observers, on a bitter Bible reading in the public schools case shortly after the Civil War.

Blanshard, Paul. Religion and the Schools. Beacon, Boston, 1963.
A thorough summary of an exceedingly divisive issue, from Jefferson to Kennedy. Appendices include the full texts of the 1962-63 Supreme Court decisions against compulsory prayer and Bible reading.

Boles, Donald E. The Bible, Religion and the Public Schools. Iowa State University, Ames, 1965.
A study of the court decisions affecting the question.

Boles, Donald E. The Two Swords. Iowa State University, Ames, 1967.
Commentaries on every major court decision concerning religion and education until 1966.

Bower, William C. Church and State in Education. University of Chicago, Chicago, 1944.
How the two entities interact and conflict in the schoolroom.

Bower, William C. Moral and Spiritual Values in Education. University of Kentucky, Lexington, 1952.
A report on the first three years of the Kentucky experiment in teaching moral values in the public school framework.

Braiterman, Marvin. Religion and the Public Schools. New York, 1958.
A significant Jewish viewpoint.

Brown, Samuel Windsor. The Secularization of American Education. Columbia University Press, New York, 1912. (reprint AMS Press, New York, 1972).
A survey of court decisions and legislative enactments leading to a secularization of education.

Brubacher, John S., ed. The Public Schools and Spiritual Values. Harper, New York, 1944.
A defense of the naturalistic approach to religion in state schools by a group of eminent educators.

Butts, R. Freeman. The American Tradition in Religion and Education. Beacon, Boston, 1950.
A study showing the relation between public education, religious voluntarism, and freedom.

CHURCH, STATE AND EDUCATION

Byrnes, Lawrence. <u>Religion and Public Education</u>. Harper and Row, New York, 1975.
Intended primarily for public school teachers, this is a better than average clarification of the legal, psychological and pedagogic aspects of teaching about religion in the public school context.

Clayton, A. Stafford. <u>Religion and Schooling, a Comparative Study</u>. Blaisdell, Waltham, Massachusetts, 1969.
A professor of education at Indiana University depicts religious education and the relation of religion to government schools in England, the Netherlands and Sweden. Excellent study.

Confrey, Burton. <u>Secularism in American Education - Its History</u>. Catholic University of America, Washington, D.C., 1931.
A summary of state legislation on religious instruction in public schools by one who deplores secularization.

Connors, Edward M. <u>Church-State Relationships in Education in the State of New York</u>. Catholic University of America, Washington, D.C., 1951. Comprehensive survey.

Coxe, Claire. <u>The Fourth R: What Can be Taught about Religion in the Public Schools</u>. Hawthorn, New York, 1969.
A good factual and practical guide for students, teachers, and parents.

Culver, Raymond B. <u>Horace Mann and Religion in the Massachusetts Public Schools</u>. Yale University Press, New Haven, 1929.
A study of the formative years in American public education, with particular emphasis on the role of educator Horace Mann. Author shows how traditional religionists fought tooth and nail against the secularization process.

Curran, Francis X. <u>The Churches and the Schools</u>. Loyola University, Chicago, 1954.
A fascinating study of the agonizing reappraisal on education within Nineteenth century American Protestantism. Author studied important religious journals and records of denominational meetings in which decisions favorable to the relinquishment of church control over education were taken.

Davis, Mary Dabney. <u>Week-Day Religious Instruction</u>. U.S. Government Printing Office, Washington, D.C., 1933.
Results of a 1932 survey by the Office of Education, showing that 218 out of 2,043 cities surveyed released students for religious instruction.

Davis, Mary Dabney. <u>Week-Day Classes in Religious Education</u>. U.S. Government Printing Office, Washington, D. C., 1941.
A similar survey, conducted in 1940, revealed that 488 of 3,790 cities in the U.S. had released-time programs.

72

CHURCH, STATE AND EDUCATION

Department of Elementary School Principals. Spiritual Values in the Elementary School. National Education Association, Washington, D.C. 1947.
   Descriptions of actual practices found in many schools in the immediate post war era.

Dierenfield, Richard B. Religion in American Public Schools. Public Affairs Press, Washington, D.C., 1962.
   America's best-known expert on the subject and a professor at Macalester College in St. Paul, Minnesota, presents the findings of a survey conducted in the early 1960s among several thousand school districts. The real picture of religious exercises and worship, religion in the curriculum, released-time programs, and parochial school busing, is revealed. A factually important book which includes charts and tables. (Note: More recent data have been collected by the author and published in the journal Religious Education (January-February 1973).

Dolbeare, Kenneth and Phillip Hammond. The School Prayer Decisions. University of Chicago, Chicago, 1971.
   A discussion of the difficulties in implementing and understanding important court decisions on the local level.

Douglas, William O. The Bible and the Schools. Little, Brown and Company, Boston, 1966.
   A brief but lucid defense of the Supreme Court's landmark decisions of 1962 and 1963 on compulsory religious practices in public schools.

Drinan, Robert. Religion, the Courts, and Public Policy. McGraw-Hill, New York, 1963.
   An overall look at the problem by a Jesuit educator, now a U.S. Congressman.

Drouin, Edmond G. The School Question: A Bibliography on Church-State Relationships in American Education, 1940-1960. Catholic University of America, Washington, D.C., 1963.

Duker, Sam. The Public Schools and Religion: The Legal Context. Harper, New York, 1966.
   What the law says.

Dunn, William K. What Happened to Religious Education? Johns Hopkins University Press, Baltimore, 1958.
   A documentary study of the importance of specifically Christian religious indoctrination in American public schools from 1776-1861.

Educational Policies Commission. Moral and Spiritual Values in the Public Schools. National Education Association, Washington, D.C., 1951.
   Official NEA report emphasizing religious tolerance and respect for diversity in whatever courses are developed in schools.

CHURCH, STATE AND EDUCATION

Ellis, Samuel Moore. The Bible Indispensable in Education. National
Reform Association, Pittsburgh, 1926.
A plea for continued mandatory Bible study in the public schools for
the literary and spiritual qualities allegedly received.

Engel, David E., ed. Religion in Public Education. Paulist, Paramus,
New Jersey, 1974.
A stimulating collection of essays on the legal, philosophical, and
pedagogic problems of dealing adequately with religion in a public
educational context.

Fell, Marie Leonore. The Foundations of Nativism in American Textbooks,
1783-1860. Catholic University of America, Washington, D.C., 1941.
Essential study of religious bias in U.S. schoolbooks from the
Revolution to the Civil War.

Fleming, W. S. God in Our Public Schools. National Reform Association,
Pittsburgh, 1942.
Author believes that "nonsectarian" religion in schools is essential
to block secularism, infidelity and criminality.

Freund, Paul A. and Robert Ulich. Religion and the Public Schools.
Harvard University Press, Cambridge, 1965.
An historical-legal survey.

Frommer, Arthur, ed. The Bible and the Public Schools. Frommer, New York,
1963.
Contains the Schempp case in its entirety plus excerpts from court
records and briefs.

Gobbell, L. L. Church and State Relationships in Education in North
Carolina since 1776. Duke University, Durham, 1938.
The definitive study of religion and public education in the
Tarheel State.

Gordis, Robert T., et. al. Religion and the Schools. Fund for the Republic,
Santa Barbara, 1959.
A symposium on this vital topic by prominent educators and theologians.

Gove, Floyd S. Religious Education on Public School Time. Harvard
University, Cambridge, 1926.
A survey of the nation during the mid 1920s.

Griffiths, William Edward. Religion, the Courts and the Public Schools; a
Century of Litigation. W. H. Anderson, Cincinnati, 1966.
Part of the American school law series.

Hall, Arthur Jackson. Religious Education in the Public Schools of the
State and City of New York. University of Chicago, Chicago, 1914.

CHURCH, STATE AND EDUCATION

Hall, Christopher. The Christian Teacher and the Law. Christian Legal
      Society, Box 2069, Oak Park, Illinois, 60603, 1975.
      An up-to-date survey of how far a religiously-committed teacher may
      or may not go in witnessing for a religious position in public schools.

Hauser, Conrad A. Teaching Religion in the Public School. Round Table
      Press, New York, 1942.
      An Evangelical and Reformed minister regards religion as an
      essential element for the curriculum.

Hay, C. L. The Blind Spot in American Public Education. Macmillan, New
      York, 1950.
      A critique of traditional American disinterest in religion as an
      academic discipline. Author believes that religious illiteracy is
      a serious and unresolved American problem.

Healey, Robert M. Jefferson on Religion in Public Education. Yale
      University Press, New Haven, 1962.
      Unique study, with which many may disagree.

Helmreich, Ernst C. Religion and the Maine Schools: An Historical
      Approach. Bureau for Research in Municipal Government, Brunswick,
      Maine, 1960.
      An interesting case study of changing patterns.

Henry, Virgil. The Place of Religion in Public Schools. Harper, New
      York, 1950.
      A reasonably sympathetic view which emphasizes church-state partner-
      ship in education.

Holtz, Adrian Augustus. A Study of the Moral and Religious Elements in
      American Secondary Education up to 1800. Menasha, Wisconsin, 1917.
      An exhaustive study, proving how unreservedly sectarian were schools
      in Colonial America.

Hood, William R. The Bible in the Public Schools, Legal Status and
      Current Practice. U.S. Government Printing Office, Washington, D.C.,
      1923.

Howlett, Walter Main. Religion, the Dynamic of Education. Harper, New
      York, 1929.
      The central importance of religion as an academic discipline and a
      unifying element shown.

Hubner, Sister Mary. Professional Attitudes toward Religion in the
      Public Schools of the U.S. since 1900. Catholic University of
      America, Washington, D.C., 1944.
      Valuable study.

Hurley, Mark J. Church-State Relationships in Education in California.
      Catholic University of America, Washington, D.C., 1948.

CHURCH, STATE AND EDUCATION

Jackson, Jerome Case and Constantine Malmberg. Religious Education and
the State. Doubleday, Doran, Garden City, 1928.
The problems and possibilities considered.

Johnson, Alvin W. The Legal Status of Church-State Relationships in the
U.S., with Special Reference to the Public Schools. University of
Minnesota Press, Minneapolis, 1934.
Valuable compilation.

Johnson, F. Ernest, ed. American Education and Religion. Harper, New
York, 1952.
A collection of speeches by leading authorities, prepared for the
Institute for Religious and Social Studies.

Jones, Alonzo T. The Place of the Bible in Education. Pacific Press,
Oakland, 1903.
A Seventh-day Adventist view.

Laubach, John H. School Prayers: Congress, the Courts, and the Public.
Public Affairs Press, Washington, D.C., 1969.
A comprehensive look at the school prayer question.

Little, Lawrence Calvin. Religion and Public Education; a Bibliography.
University of Pittsburgh, Pittsburgh, 1966.
Contains 3,200 items.

Loder, James E. Religion and the Public Schools. Association Press,
New York, 1965.
Study of the appropriate and inappropriate uses of religion in
public school curricula.

Lowry, Charles Wesley. To Pray or Not to Pray! University Press of
Washington, Washington, D.C., 1963.
An attempt to resolve this dilemma in a multifaith community.

McCluskey, Neil G. Public Schools and Moral Education. Columbia University
Press, New York, 1958.
A commentary on the influences of Horace Mann and John Dewey on
American public education, particularly as related to the inculcation
of moral values.

McCollum, Vashti. One Woman's Fight. Doubleday, New York, 1951.
A personal memoir by a courageous humanist who objected to obligatory
religious exercises and shared time programs in Illinois public
schools. Her objections resulted in a favorable U.S. Supreme Court
decision.

McCormick, Leo Joseph. Church-State Relationships in Education in
Maryland. Catholic University of America, Washington, D.C., 1942.

Madden, Ward. Religious Values in Education. Harper, New York, 1951.
Author maintains that ethical dimensions can permeate the public

school without violating secratian sensibilities.

Mahoney, Charles J. The Relation of the State to Religious Education in Early New York 1633-1825. Catholic University of America, Washington, D.C., 1941.

Marcus, Lloyd. The Treatment of Minorities in Secondary School Textbooks. Anti-Defamation League, New York, 1961.
A criticism of the Protestant, Anglo-Saxon view of reality which permeates, in the author's view, American texts.

Mason, Robert E. Moral Values and Secular Education. Columbia University Press, New York, 1950.
An attempt to define limits and parameters within which secular education can legitimately appraise and foster moral values.

Mead, Edwin D. The Roman Catholic Church and the Public Schools. George H. Ellis, Boston, 1890.
A critique of Catholic efforts to de-Protestantize the public schools.

Michaelsen, Robert. Piety in the Public School. Macmillan, New York, 1970.
Excellent historical survey of religion's role in American public education.

Moehlman, Conrad H. The Church as Educator. Hinds, Hayden and Eldridge, New York, 1947.
The church should develop sound religious education programs without recourse to the state.

Moehlman, Conrad H. School and Church, the American Way. Harper, New York, 1944.
Sympathetic look at public education plus a statement against overt sectarianism in public schools.

Moore, Opal. Why Johnny Can't Learn. Mott Media, Milford, Michigan, 1975.
A poorly-documented incoherent attack on alleged atheism, subversion and secular humanism in public schools.

Muir, William K. Prayer in the Public Schools. University of Chicago, Chicago, 1967. (new 1973 edition renamed Law and Attitude Change)
A survey of 28 school administrators, showing how difficult it is to change deeply held attitudes.

National School Public Relations Association. Religion and the Schools. Washington, D. C., 1970.
A brief survey of church-state problems in the field of education.

Nations, Gilbert O. Roman Catholic War on Public Schools. Independent Publishing Company, Washington, D.C., 1931.
Purports to be a collection of Vatican and local Catholic hierarchy documents condemning free public, secular education. Urges government to abolish all private schools.

CHURCH, STATE AND EDUCATION

Newman, Louis. The Sectarian Invasion of Our Public Schools. San Francisco, 1925.
A rabbi presents considerable documentary evidence to show that Protestant fundamentalists and evangelicals succeeded in "capturing" American public schools by many methods, subtle and overt. Newman calls for absolute religious neutrality on the part of public educational institutions.

Nielsen, Niels C. God in Education: A New Opportunity for American Schools. Sheed and Ward, New York, 1966.
A Protestant educator persuasively defends the objective study of religion.

O'Neill, James M. The Catholic in Secular Education. Longmans, Green and Company, New York, 1956.
A plea for serious Catholic involvement in public schools and colleges by a Catholic devoted to strengthening public education.

O'Neill, James M. Religion and Education under the Constitution. Harper, New York, 1949.
A Catholic public school educator interprets the Constitution in an elastic way which would allow some cooperation between church and state in education.

Panoch, James U. and David L. Barr. Religion Goes to School. Harper and Row, New York, 1968.
An impressive compilation of materials suitable for academic religion courses in public schools, though at least one critic, Robert Michaelsen, regarded them as "designed primarily for religious education in a religious context".

Phenix, Philip H. Religious Concerns in Contemporary Education. Columbia University, New York, 1959.
The dean of Carleton College discusses the relation of religion to the school, teacher, curriculum and administrative process.

Politella, Joseph. Religion in Education: An Annotated Bibliography. Oneonta, New York, 1956.

Rainey, George S. Bibles in the Public Schools; or, a Plea for Religious Liberty. Otterbein, Indiana, 1924.
A plea for religious harmony.

Raywid, Mary Anne. The Ax-Grinders; Critics of Our Public Schools. Macmillan, New York, 1962.
Author exposes and rejects the sweeping generalization that American public education is inherently irreligious.

Rian, Edwin H. Christianity and American Education. Naylor, San Antonio, Texas, 1949.
Lucid historical essay on public, Roman Catholic and Protestant

education in America, by one who urges more religion in all educational curricula.

Rice, Charles E. The Supreme Court and Public Prayer. Fordham University, New York, 1964.
A conservative Roman Catholic law professor maintains that nonsectarian public prayer is still licit, despite U.S. Supreme Court rulings.

School Prayers. Hearings before the Committee on the Judiciary, House of Representatives, Eighty-Eighth Congress, on Proposed Amendments to the Constitution Relating to Prayers and Bible Reading in the Public Schools. U.S. Government Printing Office, Washington, D.C., 1964.

Sellers, Horace B. The Constitution and Religious Education. Boston, 1950.

Sizer, Theodore R., ed. Religion and Public Education. Houghton-Mifflin, Boston, 1967.
A typical anthology.

Spear, Samuel Thayer. Religion and the State; or, The Bible and the Public Schools. Dodd, Mead, New York, 1876.
A defense of compulsory Bible reading.

Spurlock, Clark. Education and the Supreme Court. University of Illinois, Urbana, 1955.
A survey of all major decisions, including those affecting church and state.

Steiner, Franklin. The Bible: Should it be in the School Room? The Question considered Legally, Morally, and Religiously. Haldeman-Julius, Girard, Kansas, 1924.
A secular humanist approach.

Swomley, John M. Religion, the State and the Schools. Pegasus, New York, 1968.
A consideration of the major church-state issues from a staunch separationist perspective.

Thayer, V. T. The Attack upon the American Secular School. Beacon, Boston, 1951.
A rebuttal to those critics who have charged that U.S. public schools are inherently hostile to religion. Author contends that neutrality in religion is the only approach consistent with democracy.

Thayer, V. T. Public Education and its Critics. Macmillan, New York, 1954.
Continuing the line he developed in his previous book, Thayer defends American public education and calls it a unique success story.

Thayer, V.T. Religion in Public Education. Viking, New York, 1947.
Constitutional and academic problems bared.

CHURCH, STATE AND EDUCATION

Towns, Elmer. *Have the Public Schools Had It?* Nelson, Nashville, 1974.
A jeremiad against public education and a call for both reintroducing religious indoctrination in public schools and developing a separate Christian school system. Lamentably,many factual errors abound.

Van Dusen, Henry P. *God in Education*. Scribners, New York, 1951.
Author tries to develop a synthesis which can integrate moral values into education without engaging in indoctrination.

Wilder, Amos N., ed. *Liberal Learning and Religion*. Harper, New York, 1951.
Fifteen scholars deal with the difficulty of preserving academic freedom and, at the same time, of dealing adequately with religion.

Williams, J. Paul. *The New Education and Religion*. Association Press, New York, 1945.
A defense of the thesis that teaching about religion is essential for a balanced education. Contains many suggested solutions and a survey of how religious education is handled in other nations.

Winchester, Benjamin Severance. *Religious Education and Democracy*.
Abingdon, New York, 1917.
Author believes the two are interrelated.

Chapter VII

THE VATICAN AS A FACTOR IN CHURCH-STATE RELATIONS

Unquestionably the Vatican has been a major influence in western civilization for most of the past twenty centuries. Its influence on the development of western law and diplomacy is incalculable, and books in this chapter treat both sympathetically and critically the Vatican's role in church-state relations.

Ambrosini, Maria Luisa. The Secret Archives of the Vatican. Little Brown, Boston, 1969.
Fascinating excursion; valuable for specialists.

Arthur, William. The Popes, the Kings and the People; a History of the Movement to Make the Pope Governor of the World. Hodder and Stoughton, London, 1877. (revised 1903).
Critical of Vatican policies.

Babis, Daniel G. and Anthony J. Maceli. A United States Ambassador to the Vatican. Pageant Press, New York, 1952.
A brief Roman Catholic defense of the possible exchange of ambassadors between the U.S. and the Holy See.

Bagnani, Gilbert. Rome and the Papacy: An Essay on the Relations between Church and State. Methuen, London, 1929.
A moderately critical and highly informative disquisition on the Vatican's role in church-state conflict.

Barrett, E. Boyd. While Peter Sleeps. Ives Washburn, New York, 1929.
A plea for reform in the Vatican by an ex-Jesuit psychologist.

Behn, Ernst. The Papacy Evaluated. Northwest, Milwaukee, 1962.
Highly critical Lutheran study.

Bernhart, J. The Vatican as a World Power. Longmans-Green, New York, 1939.
Objective and informative analysis.

Bokun, Branko. Spy in the Vatican 1941-45. Praeger, New York, 1973.
The diary of a Yugoslavian Red Cross worker sent to Rome to plead with the Vatican to use its influence to stop the Croatian massacre.

Brezzi, Paolo. The Papacy: Its Origins and Historical Evolution. Newman, Westminster, Maryland, 1958.
A study of the nature and purpose, and political role of the Papacy in Western culture.

Bull, George. Vatican Politics at the Second Vatican Council. Oxford University, New York, 1966.
The Royal Institute of International Affairs' valuable study of the political implications of the great synod.

Butler, C. M. Inner Rome: Political, Religious and Social. Lippincott, Philadelphia, 1866.

a denunciation of Papal rule in the last days of the Papal States.

Cathcart, William. The Papal System. Philadelphia, 1872.
Massive critique.

Cavallari, Alberto. The Changing Vatican. Doubleday, Garden City, 1967.
An Italian journalist's "inside" view of the Vatican, including an
interview with Pope Paul himself.

Cianfarra, Camille M. The Vatican and the War. Dutton, New York, 1945.
A sympathetic assessment of the Vatican's role.

Cianfarra, Camille M. The Vatican and the Kremlin. Dutton, New York, 1950.
Analysis of postwar conflict between the superpowers.

"Civis Romanus". The Pope is King. Putnams, New York and London, 1929.
Immensely useful study of the Vatican 1870-1929, including the full
text of the Lateran Pacts.

Collette, C. H. The Papacy. London, 1885.
Unfavorable assessment.

Corbett, James A. The Papacy. Van Nostrand, Princeton, New Jersey, 1956.
A brief historical account with emphasis on political questions.

Crowley, Jeremiah. The Pope - Chief of White Slaves, High Priest of Intrigue.
Wheaton, Illinois, 1913.
An ex-priest's emotional tirade.

Daim, Wilfried. The Vatican and Eastern Europe. Frederick Ungar, New York,
1970.
The only up-to-date evaluation of Vatican policy toward each Soviet
bloc nation. Originally published in Vienna in 1967.

De Cesare, R. Last Days of Papal Rome. Boston, 1909.
Anti-Papal account of the fall of the Papal States.

Denny, Edward. Papalism. Rivington, London, 1912.
Unfavorable study of Vatican political philosophy.

Eckhardt, Carl Conrad. The Papacy and World Affairs as Reflected in the
Secularization of Politics. University of Chicago, Chicago, 1937.

Falconi, Carlo. The Silence of Pius XII. Little, Brown, Boston, 1969.
Controversial documentary on Pius's political and diplomatic moves.

Farago, Ladislas. Aftermath: Martin Borman and the Fourth Reich.
Simon and Schuster, New York, 1974.
Contains a devastating section, pages 167-198, on the pro-Nazi
activities of high Vatican officialdom, led by Bishop Alois Hudal.

THE VATICAN AS A FACTOR IN CHURCH-STATE RELATIONS

Farrow, John. Pageant of the Popes. Sheed and Ward, New York, 1950.
(All Saints, New York, 1965, paper)
A narrative history of exceptional merit.

Fremantle, Anne, ed. The Papal Encyclicals in their Historic Context.
Mentor-Omega, New York, 1956.
An excellent anthology of Papal encyclicals through twenty centuries,
with contextual interpretation by Ms. Fremantle.

Friedlander, Saul. Pius XII and The Third Reich. Alfred A Knopf, New
York, 1966.
A critical study of the Pope's alleged sympathy for the Axis powers.

Gladstone, William E. Rome and the Newest Fashions in Religion. London,
1875. The Vatican Decrees in their Bearing on Civil Allegiance.
London, 1874. Vaticanism. London, 1875.
Three highly unfavorable studies of Vatican policy by Britain's
liberal Prime Minister.

Gohdes, C. B. Does the Modern Papacy Require a New Evaluation? Lutheran
Literary Board, Burlington, Iowa, 1940.
Critical study which lacks cohesion.

Gonella, Guido. The Papacy and World Peace. Hollis and Carter, London,
1945.
The influence of the Vatican on postwar peace settlements considered.

Graebner, Theodore. The Pope and Temporal Power. Northwest, Milwaukee,
1929.
Critical Lutheran analysis.

Graham, Robert A. The Rise of the Double Diplomatic Corps in Rome.
Martinus Nihjoff, The Hague, Holland. 1952.
A study of Vatican diplomacy and its influence on Western political
history.

Graham, Robert A. Vatican Diplomacy. Princeton University Press, Princeton,
1959.
Still the definitive survey of Vatican diplomatic initiatives through
history by an American Jesuit who is presently editing the Vatican's
World War II documents. Thorough and scholarly.

Guerry, Emile. The Popes and World Government. Helicon, Baltimore-
Dublin, 1964.
An exposition of Papal teaching on the international order, the
community of nations, and the rights and duties of civil states.

Gwynn, Denis Rolleston. The Vatican and War in Europe. Burns and Oates,
London, 1940.
A sympathetic Irish journalist's interpretation.

THE VATICAN AS A FACTOR IN CHURCH-STATE RELATIONS

Hershey, Scott. The Roman Papacy. Boston, 1895.
Typically hostile Nativist document.

Heston, Edward L. The Holy See at Work. Bruce, Milwaukee, 1950.
The administrative and persuasive elements of the Vatican portrayed.

Hoare, F. R. The Papacy and the Modern State. Burns and Oates, London,
1940.
Sympathetic study.

Hochhuth, Rolf. The Deputy. Grove Press, New York, 1964.
The devastating play which charges Pope Pius XII with complicity in
the Nazi holocaust for his failure to speak out against the savage
persecutions of the Jews. Author documents his charges in a historical
essay appended to the text. See also The Storm Over the Deputy, edited
by Robert Bentley, Grove Press, New York, 1964, for a scintillating
collection of essays on the issues raised by Hochhuth.

Hollis, Christopher, ed. The Papacy. Macmillan, New York, 1964.
The one-time British member of Parliament brings together essays by
twenty-six European and American scholars on the role of the Papacy
in Western political and cultural life.

Hughes, Philip. The Pope's New Order. Macmillan, New York, 1944.
A noted British Catholic historian systematically interprets the
social and political encyclicals of Popes Leo XIII, Pius X, Benedict XV,
Pius XI and Pius XII.

Johnson, Humphrey J. T. Vatican Diplomacy in the World War. Blackwell,
Oxford, 1933.
An objective account of the First World War.

Kauffman, Luther S. Romanism as a World Power. True American Publishing
Company, Philadelphia, 1922.
A critical indictment of Vatican politics in the form of a lengthy
address delivered on December 12, 1921 in Philadelphia.

Kerr, William Shaw. A Handbook on the Papacy. Marshall Morgan and Scott,
London, 1950.
A critique of Papal claims by a Church of Ireland bishop.

Lehmann, Leo H. Behind the Dictators. Agora, New York, 1944.
Vatican Policy in the Second World War. Agora, New York, 1946.
Accuses the Papacy of sympathizing with Fascism before and during
World War II. Reasonably well documented.

Leo XIII, Pope. The Church Speaks to the Modern World. Edited by Etienne
Gilson. Doubleday Image, New York, 1954.
The notable French philosopher Gilson presents an annotated collection
of the social and political encyclicals of Pope Leo XIII from 1878 to
1903. Included are several dealing with church and state and religious
liberty, e.g. Libertas Praestantissimum, Diuturnum, Immortale Dei,

THE VATICAN AS A FACTOR IN CHURCH-STATE RELATIONS

Rerum Novarum, Sapientiae Christianae, and Graves de Communi.

Levitt, Albert. Vaticanism: The Political Principles of the Roman Catholic Church. Vantage, New York, 1960.
An unfavorable assessment of Vatican policies.

Loeppert, Adam J. Modernism and the Vatican. Jennings and Graham, Cincinnati and New York, 1912.
An unfavoralbe look at Vatican attempts to stamp out Modernism in seven countries as well as at The Holy See.

Loisy, Alfred. My Duel with the Vatican. New York, 1949.
The French Modernist's inside view.

Man, E. Garnet. Papal Aims and Papal Claims. Swan Sonnenschein, London, 1902.
A critical look at Papal history.

Manhattan, Avro. Catholic Imperialism and World Freedom. Watts, London, 1952 (revised 1959).
Highly unfavorable judgment.

Manhattan, Avro. The Dollar and the Vatican. Pioneer, London, 1956.
A bitter criticism of the entente between the Vatican and the U.S.A. in the days of Pius XII, Eisenhower, Dulles and Cardinal Spellman.

Manhattan, Avro. The Vatican in World Politics. Horizon, New York 1949. Watts, London, 1947 (under title The Catholic Church Against the Twentieth Century).
A critical documentary on Vatican political policies by one who believes the Vatican sympathized with Fascism in order to Catholicize the world.

Manhattan, Avro. Vatican Imperialism in the Twentieth Century. Zondervan, Grand Rapids, 1965.
An elaboration on the author's earlier books, including the Vietnam fracas.

Mary Claudia, Sister. A Dictionary of Papal Pronouncements. Kenedy, New York, 1958.
A valuable reference work, this volume includes excerpts from Papal encyclicals, letters, and allocutions from 1878 to 1957. The entries are arranged alphabetically by subject.

McCabe, Joseph. The Papacy in Politics Today. Watts, London, 1937. (revised 1943)
An indictment of alleged Vatican support for Fascist totalitarianism.

MacGregor, Geddes. The Vatican Revolution. Beacon, Boston, 1957.
Study of Vatican policy since Pope Pius IX with primary emphasis on the consequences of the Infallibility decree.

THE VATICAN AS A FACTOR IN CHURCH-STATE RELATIONS

McGurn, Barrett. A Reporter Looks at the Vatican. Coward-McCann, New York, 1962.
Informed narrative by an observant journalist.

McKnight, John P. The Papacy. Rinehart, New York, 1952.
An objective overview by a Presbyterian journalist.

Micklem, Nathaniel. Papalism and Politics. Independent Press, London, 1955.
Brief, critical look at political influence of the church under Pius XII.

Nations, Gilbert O. Papal Sovereignty. Cincinnati, 1917.
Critical analysis of Papal political policies.

Neuvecelle, Jean. The Vatican: Its Organization, Customs and Way of Life. Criterion, New York, 1955.
A French journalist thoroughly analyzes the Vatican in the days of Pius XII in a superbly written work.

Neville, Robert. The World of the Vatican. Harper and Row, New York, 1962.
Warm and friendly but factual portrait by a prominent journalist.

Nippold, Friedrich. The Papacy in the Nineteenth Century. Putnams, New York and London, 1900.
A translation of a superior German study of Papal policies and influences.

Paris, Edmond. The Vatican Against Europe. Protestant Truth Society, London, 1961.
A liberal French Catholic denounces alleged Vatican sympathy with Fascism.

Pastor, Ludwig Von. The History of the Popes. 40 volumes. Herder, St. Louis, 1915-1938.
A monumental historical classic by a German historiographer, covering the years 1305 to 1799. Pastor was once Austrian ambassador to the Holy See.

Pepper, Curtis G. The Pope's Back Yard. Farrar, Straus and Giroux, New York, 1967.
An engaging portrait of the Vatican by a Newsweek reporter.

Pichon, Charles. The Vatican and Its Role in World Affairs. Dutton, New York, 1950.
Thoroughly objective study.

Pigott, Adrian. Freedom's Foe - The Vatican. Wickliffe Press, London, 1956. The Vatican Versus Mankind. Wickliffe Press, London, 1964.
A rationalist's unfavorable assessment.

Pius XI, Pope. The Church and the Reconstruction of the Modern World. ed. Terence P. McLaughlin. Doubleday Image, New York, 1957.

THE VATICAN AS A FACTOR IN CHURCH-STATE RELATIONS

The social and political encyclicals of the Pope who reigned during the crucial inter-war years, 1923-1938.

Pius XII, Pope. The Pope Speaks. ed. Michael Chinigo. Pantheon, New York, 1957.
A collection of the major pronouncements of Pius XII, who frequently dealt with political and social issues.

Raynor, Frank C. The Giant Masquerade. Morgan and Scott, London, 1926.
Hostile survey of the Papacy's political and cultural influence throughout history.

Rhodes, Anthony B. The Vatican in the Age of the Dictators, 1922-1945. Holt, Rinehart and Winston, New York, 1974.
Immensely scholarly and highly sympathetic account of Vatican policies during a crucial epoch of history. Essential reading.

Ridley, F. A. The Papacy and Fascism. Watts, London, 1938. (reprint APM, New York, 1973).
Generally unfavorable assessment of Vatican attempts at neutrality.

Ryan, Alvan S., ed. Newman and Gladstone: The Vatican Decrees. University Of Notre Dame, Notre Dame, 1962.
Collection of correspondence and essays on the civil and political implications of the decrees of the First Vatican Council.

Scottish Protestant Alliance. The Papacy of Modern Times. Glasgow, 1886.
A collection of essays and addresses on growing Papal political influence throughout Europe. Anti-Papal.

Seldes, George. The Catholic Crisis. Julian Messner, New York, 1939. (revised edition 1945).
A look at the tension between democracy and authoritarianism in the Vatican. Excellent.

Seldes, George. The Vatican: Yesterday, Today, Tomorrow. Harper, New York, 1934.
A superb study of the Vatican by a literate journalist who has never really been surpassed by recent Vaticanologists.

Sencourt, Robert. The Genius of the Vatican. Jonathan Cape, London, 1935.
Brilliant study of Papal diplomacy and political influence.

Shotwell, J. T. and L. R. Loomis. The See of Peter. Columbia University Press, New York, 1927.
Historical portrait.

Sweeney, Francis, ed. Vatican Impressions. Sheed and Ward, New York, 1962.
A delightful anthology by admirers and critics through two centuries. Unexcelled.

THE VATICAN AS A FACTOR IN CHURCH-STATE RELATIONS

Teeling, William. The Pope in Politics. Lovat Dickson, London, 1937.
    A liberal Catholic analysis of the pontificate of Pius XI.

Thompson, Richard Wigginton. The Papacy and the Civil Power. Nelson and
    Philips, New York, 1872.
    A brilliant discourse on the political and diplomatic relationship
    between the Papacy and civil governments. Author was Secretary of
    the Navy under President Hayes.

Ullmann, Walter. The Growth of Papal Government in the Middle Ages.
    London, 1962.
    A good historical treatise on the rise of the Papacy from the Fifth
    Century to the Reformation.

Van Lierde, Peter C. The Holy See at Work. Hawthorn, New York, 1962.
    An account of the administrative machinery of the Vatican by a
    Dutch bishop who was an official of the Curia for many years.

Von Aretin, Karl Otmar. The Papacy and the Modern World. McGraw-Hill,
    New York, 1970. Weidenfeld and Nicholson, London, 1970.
    One of the best works in the field. Readable and filled with charts,
    maps, chronological tables and excellent bibliography.

Wall, Bernard. Report on the Vatican. Harper, New York, 1955. London, 1956
    An excellent study of the political importance of the Vatican in the
    1950s by an outstanding journalist.

Wallace, Lillian Parker. The Papacy and European Diplomacy. University of
    North Carolina, Chapel Hill, 1948.
    Admirable historical analysis.

Wartime Correspondence between President Roosevelt and Pope Pius XII. Intro-
    duction by Myron C. Taylor. Macmillan, New York, 1947.
    Fairly useful documentary. Avoids controversy.

Wells, H. G. Crux Ansata. Agora, New York, 1944. Penguin, London, 1944.
    Wells' last book, subtitled "an indictment of the Roman Catholic Church"
    for its pro-Fascist policies.

Wylie, J. A. The Papacy, Its History, Dogmas, Genius and Prospects.
    Andrew Elliot, Edinburgh and Hamilton, Adams, and Company, London,
    1852 (revised 1889).
    A scholarly critique.

Wylie, J. A. Rome and Civil Liberty, or the Papal Aggression. London, 1864.
    Which Sovereign, Queen Victoria or the Pope? The Protestant Alliance,
    London, 1870.
    Critical studies of Vatican politics.

Yates, Gerard F., ed. Papal Thought on the State. Appleton, New York, 1958.
    A collection of essays on Papal church-state thought.

Chapter VIII

RELIGIOUS CONTROVERSY

Closely related to religious conflict is the persistence of religious controversy. Books in this chapter will consist primarily of writings dealing with the understanding which Protestants and Catholics have held of each other's faiths. A whole body of expository literature has been developed in the last century-and-a-half relating to the theme of the compatibility or incompatibility of Roman Catholicism and republican institutions. A large number of books dealing with this question will be considered here because the climate in which laws relating to religion are or were formulated has often been deeply affected by religious polemic.

One section of this chapter may be a bit surprising. I have included a large number of books dealing with interfaith conversions. Both Roman Catholics and Protestants actively sought the conversion of members of the opposite group to their faiths. The persistence of this hostility even within members of the same basic religion was a sign of tension and misunderstanding which often affected the outcome of church-state relations at a given time in history. Indeed, in some nations proselytism was actively forbidden. One can note Spain and Greece in recent times though Greece has an immeasurably worse record. Hindu Nepal prohibits conversion from one faith to another and punishes such conversion in its criminal code. Thus we see that active attempts at conversion may often influence civil law just as conflict surrounding alleged horrors in convents often led state legislatures in the Nineteenth and early Twentieth Centuries to impose a rigid convent inspection law.

Bitter attacks on parochial schools led the Oregon legislature to petition a referendum in 1922 which would in effect have abrogated all private or parochial schools in that state. This referendum was approved by Oregon voters but was subsequently nullified by the U. S. Supreme Court. Also included in this chapter are books stemming from the ecumenical movement, which indicate a change in interfaith perception and thus an improvement in church-state relations.

I have not annotated every selection in this section, as in others, if the title or subtitle is self-explanatory or if there is a great similarity in the titles. In the interfaith conversion area, there is a distinct sameness to much of the literature.

A. Interfaith Conversion to Catholicism

Adams, Elizabeth Laura. Dark Symphony. Sheed and Ward, New York, 1942.

Allies, Thomas William. A Life's Decision. London, 1880.
    A prominent Roman Catholic convert looks back on his life in this
    lengthy autobiography and concludes that his conversion was a sound
    decision, evoking no regrets.

Angell, Charles and Charles La Fontaine. Prophet of Reunion. Seabury,
    New York, 1975.

An engaging and informative portrait of Father Paul of the Graymoor
Friars and how his conversion from the Episcopal to the Roman
Catholic Church affected interfaith relations and ecumenical
endeavors.

Anson, Peter Frederick. A Roving Recluse. Mercier, Cork, 1946.
Memoirs of a talented and prolific author.

Armstrong, April Ousler. House with a Hundred Gates. McGraw-Hill, New
York, 1965.

Baker, Gladys. I Had to Know. Appleton, New York, 1951.
An exceptionally literate conversion account, by a prominent foreign
correspondent.

Ballantyne, Murray. All or Nothing. Sheed and Ward, New York, 1956.

Barreau, Jean Claude. The Faith of a Pagan. Paulist, New York, 1968.

Barres, Oliver. One Shepherd, One Flock. Sheed and Ward, New York, 1956.
A Congregationalist minister relates the story of the conversion of
his family and himself to Rome.

Benson, Robert Hugh. Confessions of a Convert. Longmans, London, 1913.
Son of a prominent Archbishop of Canterbury became a fiery convert
to Catholicism and an imaginative novelist.

Brownson, Orestes Augustus. The Convert. Sadlier, New York, 1885.
Views of one of the most prominent Nineteenth Century converts.

Budenz, Louis. This is my Story. Browne and Nolan, Dublin, 1948.
Whittlesey House, New York, 1947.
A former Communist propagandist took a long road before arriving
at the Eternal City.

Burnett, Peter Hardeman. The Path Which Led a Protestant Lawyer to the
Catholic Church. Benziger, New York, 1859. (reprint Herder,
St. Louis, 1921)

Burton, Naomi. More than Sentinels. Doubleday, Garden City, 1964.

Carrel, Alexis. The Voyage to Lourdes. Harper, New York, 1950.

Cavanaugh, Arthur. My Own Backyard. Doubleday, Garden City, 1962.

Chesterton, Gilbert Keith. The Catholic Church and Conversion. New York,
London, 1927.
The great English man of letters analyses the problems, difficulties
and ultimate joys attending conversion to Catholicism.

Chesterton, Gilbert Keith. The Thing. (reprint) Sheed and Ward, New York,

1957.
Chesterton took many years to make his final decision on conversion and tells why and how he did it.

Cory, Herbert E. The Emancipation of a Free Thinker. Bruce, Milwaukee, 1941.
A comparative religion scholar carefully investigated all of the world's religious alternatives before deciding on Catholicism. Challenging.

Crosnier, Alexis. Latter-day Converts. McVey, Philadelphia, 1912.
Portraits of French converts, primarily from the ranks of humanists and athiests. (Translated from the French).

Curtis, Georgina P. Beyond the Road to Rome. Herder, St.Louis, 1914.
Sketches of sixty-two prominent Catholic converts, with an emphasis on the post-conversion growth in spiritual maturity.

Curtis, Georgina P. Some Roads to Rome in America. Herder, St. Louis, 1925.
An anthology of portraits of forty-eight American converts to the fold.

Day, Dorothy. From Union Square to Rome. Preservation of the Faith Press, 1938.
The well known social activist and founder of the Catholic Worker Movement,found in the social doctrine of the church an answer to her quest for Utopia.

Day, Helen Caldwell. Color Ebony. Sheed and Ward, New York, 1951.

Delany, Selden Peabody. Why Rome? Dial Press, New York, 1930.
The Harvard-educated blueblood who was for many years pastor of the famed Episcopal Church of St. Mary the Virgin in New York defends Rome as the seat of unity in this well-written apologia.

Dorsey, Theodore Hooper. From a Far Counrty . Our Sunday Visitor, Huntington, 1939.

Driscoll, Annette S. Literary Convert Women. Magnificat Press, Manchester, New Hampshire, 1928.
A unique look at one class of convert, the talented female writer.

Dulles, Avery. A Testimonial to Grace. Sheed and Ward, New York, 1946.
The brilliant Harvard-educated son of Eisenhower's Secretary of State, John Foster Dulles, a prominent Presbyterian himself, gives his reasons for conversion. Dulles became a Jesuit priest and professor now teaching at Catholic University of America.

Eberhard, Martin J. God's Ways are Wonderful. Randall, St. Paul, 1905.

Eustace, Cecil John. House of Bread. Longmans Green, New York, 1943.

RELIGIOUS CONTROVERSY

Gamble, Anna Dill. _My Road to Rome_. Baltimore, 1917.

Graef, Hilda. _From Fashions to the Fathers_. Newman, Westminster, 1957.
A worldly, sybaritic young lady finds meaning and purpose in life from her conversion to Catholicism.

Grant, Dorothy Fremont. _What Other Answer?_ Bruce, Wilwaukee, 1943.

Griffiths, Bede. _The Golden String_. Kenedy, New York, 1954. Harvill, London, 1954.

Hardt, Karl, ed. _We Are Now Catholics_. Newman, Westminster, 1959.
Four German Lutheran pastors give testimonies to their conversion. The editor's splendid introductory essay "Protestant-Catholic relations in German history" makes the book more useful than most in this genre.

Hasley, Lucile. _Reproachfully Yours_. Sheed and Ward, New York, 1949.
Delightful essay.

Hayes, Alice Jeannette. _A Convert's Reason Why_. Riverside, Cambridge, 1911.

Hilliard, Marion Pharo. _The Gracious Years_. St. Anthony Guild, Paterson, 1936.

Hitchcock, George S. _A Pilgrim of Eternity_. Herder, St. Louis, 1912.

Hoffman, Ross J. _Restoration_. Sheed and Ward, New York, 1934.
A profound historical study rather than a mere conversion account.

Houselander, Frances Caryll. _A Rocking Horse Catholic_. Sheed and Ward, New York, 1955.

Hulme, Kathryn Cavarly. _Undiscovered Country_. Little, Brown, Boston, 1966.

Huntington, Joshua. _Gropings after Truth_. Catholic Publication Society, New York, 1858.

Hyde, Douglas A. _I Believed_. Putnam, New York, 1950.
A former editor of the London _Daily Worker_ and a Communist agitator moved across the spectrum to a faith he once despised.

Ineson, George. _Community Journey_. Sheed and Ward, New York, 1956.
A Methodist convert to Catholicism's diary of his spiritual journey.

Iswolsky, Helene. _Light Before Dusk_. Longmans Green, New York, 1942.
Intellectually stimulating account of a Russian emigre in France during the 1920s and 1930s.

Ives, Levi Silliman. _The Trials of a Mind on its Progress to Catholicism_.

Patrick Donahue, Boston, 1854.
Author was the first Episcopalian bishop to defect to Rome.

James, Bruno Scott. Asking for Trouble. Harper, New York, 1963.

Jeffries, Betty Jean. From the Other Side. Bruce, Milwaukee, 1955.

Johnson, Vernon. One Lord, One Faith. London, 1929. (new edition by
Sheed and Ward, London, 1973).
A very popular and widely read account of an Anglo-Catholic's
conversion to Rome. Primarily deals with the question of authority.

Kane, George Louis. Twice Called. Bruce, Wilwaukee, 1959.

Kaye-Smith, Sheila. Three Ways Home. Harper, New York, 1937.
An English novelist, once a devout High Anglican and author of
Anglo-Catholicism, shifts her allegiance to the Church of Rome.

Kernan, William C. My Road to Certainty. McKay, New York, 1953.
An Episcopal rector's involvement in conservative political activities
convinced him that in Roman Catholicism alone was the preservation
of traditional values to be found.

Keyes, Frances Parkinson. Along a Little Way. Hawthorn, New York, 1962.

Kinsman, Frederick Joseph. Salve Mater. Longmans Green, New York, 1920.
The second Episcopal bishop of Delaware, a topflight scholar,
delineates the reasons for his shift of allegiance in a well-written
memoir.

Knox, Ronald A. A Spiritual Aeneid. Longmans, London and New York, 1918.
Sheed and Ward, New York and London, 1958 reprint.
One of England's most erudite and articulate essayists gives his
reasons for conversion to Rome. Son of an Archbishop of Canterbury
and once an Anglican priest himself, Knox limns a delightful portrait
of religious life in England from late Victorian days through the
Great War. The reprint includes a preface by novelist Evelyn Waugh.

Kobbe, Carolyn Therese. My Spiritual Pilgrimage. Devin-Adair, New York,
1935.

Kolbe, Frederick Charles. Up the Slopes of Mount Sion; a Progress from
Puritanism to Catholicism. Benziger, New York, 1924.

Lamb, George R. Roman Road. Sheed and Ward, New York, 1950.

Lamping, Severin, ed. Through Hundred Gates. Bruce, Milwaukee, 1939.
Notable converts from twenty-two lands, including Norwegian novelist
Sigrid Undset, French diplomat Paul Claudel, and Sir Shane Leslie.

Lepp, Ignace. From Karl Marx to Jesus Christ. Sheed and Ward, New York, 1958.
A French Communist relates his experiences on the road to disillusionment, rejection, and then new life in Catholicism as a priest.

Levy, Rosalie Marie. The Heavenly Road. New York, 1923. (Appendix contains list of converts from Judaism). (1962 edition called What Think You of Christ?   St. Paul Editions, Boston.)

Levy, Rosalie Marie. Judaism and Catholicism. New York, 1927.

Levy, Rosalie Marie. Thirty Years with Christ. New York, 1943.
From Judaism to Catholicism.

Leigh, Margaret Mary. The Fruit in the Seed. Sheed and Ward, New York, 1952.

Linden, James V. The Catholic Church Invites You. Herder, St. Louis, 1959.
Brief, elementary apology.

Long, Valentine, ed. They Have Seen His Star. St. Anthony Guild Press, Paterson, New Jersey, 1938.
Several famous Catholic converts are included in this sketchbook.

Lunn, Arnold. And Yet So New. Sheed and Ward, New York, 1959.
Further adventures on the road to faith and security by a delightful English apologist.

Lunn, Arnold. Now I See. New York, London, 1930. (1950 reprint).
A great English skiing expert and author's spiritual aeneid.

Lunn, Arnold. Within That City. Sheed and Ward, New York, 1936.
Apologetic essays on many topics.

MacGillivray, George John. Through the East to Rome. Benziger, New York, 1932.

Manning, Henry Edward (Cardinal). The Religion of a Traveler. San Francisco 1897. (Alternate title – Why I Became a Catholic)

Mannix, Edward J. American Convert Movement. Devin-Adair, New York, 1923.
A fascinating psychological study of the many routes which individuals travel to reach the ultimate goal - Rome. Author classifies the psychological typologies of conversion after a careful study of 125 years of writings by various converts. Includes extensive bibliographies of convert writings in periodicals as well as books.

Maritain, Raissa. We Have Been Friends Together. Longmans, New York, 1942.
Adventures in Grace. Longmans, New York, 1945.
Two remarkable autobiographical documents by the wife of philosopher Jacques Maritain. The Maritains, both talented authors, moved from Protestantism to skepticism to Catholicism.

RELIGIOUS CONTROVERSY

Merton, Thomas. <u>The Seven Storey Mountain</u>. Harcourt, New York, 1948.
Immensely popular for literary reasons alone, this modest best-
seller of 1948 is a classic of convert literature by an author who
became the world's most famous Trappist monk.

Moody, John. <u>The Long Road Home</u>. Macmillan, New York, 1936.
Prominent American industrialist's views.

Mould, Daphne. <u>The Rock of Truth</u>. Sheed and Ward, New York, 1953.

Mullen, James H. <u>Against the Goad</u>. Bruce, Milwaukee, 1961.

Murdick, Olin John. <u>Journey into Truth</u>. Exposition Press, New York, 1958.

Newman, John Henry (Cardinal). <u>Apologia Pro Vita Sua</u>. Many editions.
The all-time classic convert story, a summa of clarity, was originally
published in 1864 to the acclaim or ridicule of millions of Victorians.

Murray, Rosalind. <u>The Good Pagan's Failure</u>. London, New York, 1939.
The wife of famed historian Arnold Toynbee and herself an author of
some note, Mrs. Murray regarded secular humanism as insufficient to
her spiritual and intellectual needs. Hence, her fervent embrace
of the Catholic Church.

O'Brien, John A., ed. <u>Paths to Christ</u>. Our Sunday Visitor, Huntington,
Indiana, 1945.
Brief conversion testimonies by people from many walks of life with
primary emphasis on those less prominent.

<u>The Road to Damascus</u>. Doubleday, New York, 1949. (Image Books, 1955)
One of the earliest convert anthologies, this one contains testimonies
of such prominent figures as Evelyn Waugh, Fulton Oursler, Frances
Parkinson Keyes, Theodore Maynard, Robert F. Wagner and Clare Boothe
Luce.

<u>Roads to Rome</u>. Macmillan, New York, 1954 (All Saints Press, New York,
1960 paperback)
Sixteen noted converts are included in this series, including A. J.
Cronin, Bella Dodd and Anne Fremantle.

<u>The Way to Emmaus</u>. McGraw-Hill, New York, 1953.
The largest of the convert anthologies, containing thirty accounts,
this one differs from O'Brien's other collections in that these
accounts are primarily by non-spectacular, virtually unknown
individuals. Most of these contributors were either Protestant
ministers or students for the ministry.

<u>Where Dwellest Thou?</u> Gilbert Press, New York, 1956.
Twelve converts, including psychiatrist Karl Stern, actress Lillian
Roth, music critic Paul Hume, author Ronald Knox and novelist
G.B. Stern, offer brief reflections on their spiritual search.

Includes a fascinating essay from a Russian Orthodox convert, Helene Iswolsky.

Where I Found Christ. Doubleday, New York, 1950.
Another convert anthology, this one includes Katherine Burton, Dale Francis, Dorothy Day, Avery Dulles, Raissa Maritain and British member of Parliament Christopher Hollis among its fourteen contributors.

O'Brien, John A. The White Harvest; a Symposium on Methods of Convert Making. Longmans Green, New York and London, 1927.

Oddo, Gilbert L. These Came Home. Bruce, Milwaukee, 1954.
The spiritual odyssey of fifteen Catholic converts from many traditions and walks of life.

Oesterricher, John M., ed. Walls are Crumbling. Devin-Adair, New York, 1952. (Burns, London, 1953)
Seven Jewish philosophers relate their individual decisions to convert to Catholicism. Editor is a former Jew who devoted his later years to reconciliation between Judaism and Catholicism and was editor of the scholarly journal The Bridge. Contains a forward by Jacques Maritain.

Orchard, William Edwin. From Faith to Faith. Harper, New York, 1933.

Raupert, J. Godfrey, ed. Roads to Rome. Herder, St. Louis, 1908.
Personal accounts of fifty-seven late Nineteenth and early Twentieth century converts to Catholicism in England and America.

Raupert, J. Godfrey. Ten Years in Anglican Orders. Catholic Truth Society, London, 1897.

From Geneva to Rome via Canterbury. Benziger, New York, 1910.

Rebesher, Conrad F. Convert Making. Bruch, New York, 1937.
Symposium on methods.

Riach, John M. From One Convert to Another. J. S. Paluch, Chicago, 1946.

Rich, Edward Charles. Seeking the City. Burns and Oates, London, 1959.
After thirty years of service to the Church of England, this Canon of Peterborough Cathedral gave it all up for Rome.

Richards, William. On the Road to Rome. Benziger, New York, 1895.

St. Aubyn, Gwendolen. Towards a Pattern. Longmans Green, New York, 1940.

Scannell-O'Neill, D. J. Distinguished Converts to Rome in America. Herder, St. Louis, 1908.
A biographical listing, without commentary or personal testimony, of many converts.

RELIGIOUS CONTROVERSY

Scannell-O'Neill, D. J. Converts to Rome in America. Detroit, 1921.
A listing of 8,000 names, with short family history.

Schafer, Bruno. They Heard His Voice. McMullen, New York, 1952.

Shaw, Henry B. In the Shadow of Peter. St. Anthony Guild, Paterson, 1950.

Sih, Paul. From Confucius to Christ. Sheed and Ward, New York, 1952.
A Chinese convert's story.

Simon, M. Raphael. The Glory of Thy People. Macmillan, New York, 1948.
Spiritual autobiography of a brilliant Jewish psychiatrist who
entered the Roman Church in 1936 and the Trappist Order in 1940.

Stancourt, Louis Joseph. Her Glimmering Tapers. Macmillan, New York, 1943.

Stern, Gladys B. All in Good Time. Sheed and Ward, New York, 1954.

The Way it Worked Out. Sheed and Ward, New York, 1957.

Stern, Karl. The Pillar of Fire. Harcourt, Brace, New York, 1951.
Memoirs of an eminent Jewish psychiatrist.

Stoddard, John L. Rebuilding a Lost Faith. Kenedy, New York, 1922.
An exceptionally moving account of a famous travel lecturer and
writer who returned to Rome after many years an agnostic.

Twelve Years in the Catholic Church. Kenedy, New York, 1930.
Sequel to Rebuilding a Lost Faith.

Stone, James Kent. An Awakening and What Followed. Ave Maria, Notre
Dame, 1919.

Succop, Margaret Phillips. No Going Back. Academy Guild, Fresno, 1964.

Tarry, Ellen. The Third Door. David McKay, New York, 1955.

Thomson, Paul Van Kuykendall. Why I am a Catholic. Nelson, New York, 1959.
A former Episcopalian clergyman's apology.

Treacy, James J. Conquests of Our Holy Faith. Pustet, New York, 1907.
A rather triumphalistic collection of conversion stories.

Vandon, Elizabeth. Late Dawn. Sheed and Ward, New York, 1958.

Von Ruville, Albert. Back to Holy Church. Longmans Green, New York, 1911.

Ward, Maisie, ed. The English Way. Sheed and Ward, New York, 1933.
Biographical studies of noted Twentieth Century English Catholics,
edited by the renowed writer and co-founder of Sheed and Ward publishers.

Wicklow, William Cecil. *Rome is Home*. Academy Library Guild, Fresno, 1959.

Williams, Michael. *The Book of the High Romance*. Macmillan, New York, 1918.

Williamson, Hugh Ross. *The Walled Garden*. Macmillan, New York, 1957.
Michael Joseph, London, 1956.
An English novelist and essayist found Catholicism through literature.

Wu, John. *Beyond East and West*. Sheed and Ward, New York, 1951.
A Chinese attorney, once President of the International Court in
Shanghai, renounced Methodism and joined the Catholic Church in 1951.

Zolli, Eugenio. *Before the Dawn*. Sheed and Ward, New York, 1954.
Memoir of the conversion experience of the Chief Rabbi of Rome,
Israel Zoller.

B.   Interfaith Conversion from Catholicism

Abel, Theodore. *Protestant Home Missions to Catholic Immigrants*.
Institute of Social and Religious Research, New York, 1933.
An analytical inquiry, concluding that Protestant proselytizing
efforts have been moderately successful.

Aldama, Manuel. *From Roman Priest to Radio Evangelist*. Zondervan, Grand
Rapids, 1946.
The story of a Spanish convert.

Amand de Mendieta, Emmanuel. *Rome and Canterbury*. Herbert Jenkins, London,
1962.
A brilliant apologia for the "Biblical and Free Catholicism" of the
Anglican Communion by a Belgian scholar who was for thirty years a
Benedictine monk.

An Approach to Roman Catholics. The Good News Trailer Missionary
Fellowship, Wickford, Essex, England, 1961.
Offers suggestions to conversative Protestants on converting Catholics.

Arrien, Rose Fe. *A Priest Renounces Celibacy*. (also published as
I Married a Priest) Monterey Park, California, 1951. (available from
The Convert, Clairton, Pennsylvania)
A wife of an ex-priest briefly describes their marriage and his
conversion to Protestantism.

Bayssiere, Pierre. *A Letter to my Children on the Subject of my
Conversion from the Romish Church, in which I was born, to the
Protestant, in which I hope to Die*. London, 1829.

Blanchette, Charles Alphonse. *My Reasons for Leaving the Roman Catholic
Church*. Minneapolis, 1929.

Bretschneider, Karl. To Rome and Back Again. T. N. Kurtz, Baltimore, 1856.

Calhoun, S. F. Fifteen Years in the Church of Rome. Vox Populi, Lowell, Massachusetts, 1886.

Capes, John Moore. Reasons for Returning to the Church of England. Strahan, London, 1871.

Carrara, John. Out of the Wilderness. Zondervan, Grand Rapids, 1940.

Why a Preacher and not a Priest. Zondervan, Grand Rapids, 1946.

Chiniquy, Charles. Fifty Years in the Church of Rome. Revell, New York, 1886.
Perhaps the pre-eminent classic of anti-Romanism, this is the lengthy, (over 800 pages) passionate and fiery account of a French-Canadian crusader and priest who became a Protestant in 1859 and fought his former church for the remainder of his life.

Forty Years in the Church of Christ. Revell, New York, 1901. Published posthumously, this is the almost unknown sequel to "Fifty Years" and describes the author's anti-Catholic activities until his death in 1899.

Colaianni, James F., ed. Married Priests and Married Nuns. McGraw-Hill, New York, 1968.
An anthology of writings by former priests and nuns, two of whom, Edward Henriques and Victor Venete entered the Episcopal Church.

Connelly, Pierce. Reasons for Abjuring Allegiance to the See of Rome. London, 1852.
This Episcopalian clergyman converted to Rome, became disillusioned and returned to his native faith. His wife Cornelia Connelly, however, became a Roman Catholic nun.

Crowley, Jeremiah J. Romanism: A Menace to the Nation. The Menace Publishing Company, Aurora, Missouri, 1912.
A sledgehammer attack on Rome by a priest of twenty-one years.

Culleton, John. Ten Years a Priest. Louisville, Kentucky, 1893.

Cusack, M. Francis Clare. Life Inside the Church of Rome. Hodder and Stoughton, London, 1889.
A former Irish nun's critique of Rome. Author was an exceptionally talented writer and Mother-general of the Sisters of Peace. Sequel to The Nun of Kenmare.

Czechowski, Michael B. Thrilling and Instructive Developments. Boston, 1862.

Davis, Charles. A Question of Conscience. Harper and Row, New York, 1967. Hodder and Stoughton, London, 1967.

Eloquent, philosophical apologia from a man who for many years in
the 1960s was British Catholicism's theological superstar. He is
now married and teaching at McGill University in Montreal.

Dempster, Joseph S. From Romanism to Pentecost. Pentecostal Holiness
Library, Cincinnati, 1898.

Donnelly, John. Fifteen Years Behind the Curtains. Pittsburgh, 1896.
A former priest gives his "101 reasons" why he departed.

Doyle, Sir Arthur Conan. The Roman Catholic Church: A Rejoinder.
Psychic Press, London, 1930.
The creator of the immortal Sherlock Holmes left Roman Catholicism
in early manhood and moved from agnosticism to Spiritualism. When
a prominent Jesuit controversialist, Herbert Thurston, attacked
Spiritualism in a 1929 book, Doyle angrily penned this response,
which was his last work.

Duval, Francis. Reasons for Refusing to Continue a Member of the Church
of Rome. London, 1846.

Ewin, Wilson. Leading Roman Catholics to Christ. Christian Publications
Centre, Dublin, 1964.
The author has worked for many years among Roman Catholics in
Quebec and Ireland and claims to have been reasonably successful
in his conversion efforts.

Fleck, Alcyon Ruth. A Brand from the Burning. Pacific Press, Mountain
View California, 1960.
The conversion account of a Roman Catholic priest who became a
Seventh-day Adventist minister.

Gavazzi, Alessandro. Life and Lectures. DeWitt and Davenport, New York,
1853.
A famous Italian priest-orator broke with the Papacy around 1850
and toured the Protestant world, warning that Rome would endeavor to
destroy all religious liberty.

Girandola, Anthony. The Most Defiant Priest. Crown, New York, 1968.
A moving memoir of a priest who married and tried to form an independent
Catholic congregation in St. Petersburg, Florida.

Halbleib, Augustus J. The Autobiography of a Fallen Christ. Haltina,
Richmond, Virginia, 1927.

Hampel, Harry. My Deliverance from the Heresies of Rome. Dayton, Ohio,
n.d. (c.1960)

Hegger, H. T. I Saw the Light. Presbyterian and Reformed, Philadelphia,
1961.
A former Belgian Catholic gives his reasons for conversion to
conservative Protestantism.

RELIGIOUS CONTROVERSY

Houtin, Albert. The Life of a Priest. London, 1927.
Memoirs of a French modernist.

Hunkey, John. How I Became a Non-Catholic. Standard, Cincinnati, 1911.
Author became a rationalist and agnostic.

Isaacson, Charles Stuteville, ed. Roads from Rome. Religious Tract
Society, London, 1903.
A one-of-its-kind anthology of writings from thirty-seven diverse
figures who left the Roman Church in the late Nineteenth Century
and turn of the century era. Written in a relatively detatched
tone, the contributors are mostly British, French Italian or
Spanish and most seemed to have joined the Church of England, the
editor's faith.

Kavanaugh, James. A Modern Priest Looks at his Outdated Church. Trident,
New York, 1967.
A vivid critique of alleged intolerance and legalism which compelled
the author to leave the church shortly after the book's publication.

Lacueva, Francisco. From Darkness to Light. Evangelical Protestant
Society, 26 Howard Street, Belfast BT1 6PD, 1969.
Another Spanish convert to evangelical Protestantism in the early
1960s urges Rome to "return to the God of the Bible".

Leahey, Edward. Narrative of the Conversion of the Writer from Romanism
to the Christian Religion. Philadelphia, 1846.

Lehmann, Leo H. Ex-priest and the Riddle of Religion. Agora, Flushing,
New York, 1932.

The Soul of a Priest. Christ's Mission, Sea Cliff, New York, 1933.
An Irish Jesuit defects and becomes editor of the Converted Catholic
magazine. Interesting and well written account.

Longo, Gabriel. Spoiled Priest. Univetsity Books, New Hyde Park, New
York, 1966. (Paperback edition - Bantam, New York, 1967)
Disillusionment personified.

McCabe, Joseph. Twelve Years in a Monastery. C. A. Watts, London, 1930.
One of the most learned rationalists and critics of all organized
religion was once a Roman Catholic monk.

Why I Left the Church. Freethought Press Association, New York, 1897.
Succinct critique of all revealed religion, with the choicest barbs
saved for Rome.

McGerald, Samuel. Reasons Why I Cannot Return to the Church of Rome.
True Faith Company, Buffalo, 1915.

McLoughlin, Emmett. Famous Ex-Priests. Lyle Stuart, New York, 1968.
Fascinating short biographies of seventeen prominent historical

figures who left the Roman Catholic priesthood and religion. Included
are ancients like Wycliffe, Huss and Luther and more recent figures as
Doellinger, Chiniquy, Tyrrell, Loisy, Lehmann and McCabe.

People's Padre. Beacon, Boston, 1954.
A quiet best-seller, this is a moving spiritual autobiography that
impressed Reinhold Niebuhr and many other thinkers because of its
candor and forthrightness.

Malinverni, Aristide. My Conversion and Reasons That Led to It.
    Everlasting Gospel, Los Angeles, 1922.

Mayerhoffer, Vincent Philip. Twelve Years a Roman Catholic Priest.
    Rowsell and Ellis, Toronto, 1861.
    A Franciscan monk becomes a vicar in the Church of England.

Moore, John Allen, ed. Baptist Witness in Catholic Europe. Baptist
    Publishing House, Rome, 1973.
    Essays by Baptists in many Catholic lands.

Morgan, Dewi, ed. They Became Anglicans. Mowbrays, London, 1959.
    Essays on famous conversions to Anglicanism, including three
    former Roman Catholics.

O'Connor, James A. Letters to Cardinal McCloskey. "Converted Catholic"
    Publishing Office, New York, 1884.
    Angry memoirs of the founder of Christ's Mission.

O'Gorman, W. E. R. A Priest Speaks his Mind. Glendale, California, 1954.
    An Irish Protestant turned Roman Catholic priest tells why he
    returned to his childhood faith. (Privately published)

Padrosa, Luis. Why I Became a Protestant. Moody, Chicago, 1953.
    A prominent Spanish priest, psychiatrist and founder of the Loyola
    Institute converted to Protestantism in 1950 and was forced to
    leave Spain for Argentina and a seminary teaching position.

Pearson, B. H. The Monk Who Lived Again. Cowman, Los Angeles, 1940.
    A vivid account of the conversion of a Peruvian monk, Walter Montano,
    and his subsequent crusade for Protestantism in Latin America in
    the 1930s and 1940s.

Pepin, Francois. A Narrative of the Life and Experiences of Francois
    Pepin who was for more than Forty Years a Member of the Papal
    Church, Embracing an Account of his Conversion, Trials and
    Persecutions in Turning to the True Religion of the Bible. Detroit,
    1854.

Pike, James, ed. Modern Canterbury Pilgrims. Morehouse-Barlow, New York,
    1955.
    Many notable converts to the Episcopal Church, including two Roman
    Catholic priests, give their reasons.

RELIGIOUS CONTROVERSY

Poynter, J. M. Inside the Roman Church by One Who Was There. Epworth,
    London, 1930.
    A former Catholic publicist's story.

Santorio, Enrico C. Social and Religious Life of Italians in America.
    Boston, 1918.
    A commentary on the much discussed "Italian" problem of defections
    from Roman Catholicism. Protestant missionary efforts were more
    successful among this Roman Catholic ethnic group than any other.

Seguin, P. A. Out of Hell and Purgatory. Stevens Point, Wisconsin, 1912.
    Emotional account of a follower of Charles Chiniquy.

Shaughntessy, Gerald. Has the Immigrant Kept the Faith? New York, 1925.
    A much discussed sociological tract which concludes that, on the whole,
    Roman Catholicism has retained the loyalty of a majority of immigrants
    to the U.S. Author admits, however, that a rather significant number
    defected to Protestantism or indifference. Replete with statistics
    and charts.

Smith, Samuel B. Renunciation of Popery. Philadelphia, 1833.

Sullivan, William Laurence. Under Orders. Richard R. Smith, New York, 1945.
    Spiritual autobiography of a former Paulist priest who espoused
    Modernism and became a Unitarian minister and author for twenty-four
    years.

    Letters to His Holiness Pope Pius X. Open Court, Chicago, 1910.
    Though published anonymously, this was Dr. Sullivan's earliest
    rejoinder to Rome.

Vila, Manuel Perez. I Found the Ancient Way. Moody, Chicago, 1958.
    A Spanish priest finds Evangelical Protestantism irresistible.

Vinet, Lucien. I Was a Priest. Canadian Protestant League, Toronto and
    Winnipeg, 1949.
    A French Canadian priest describes his conversion and claims many
    thousands have followed him out of the Roman Church.

Von Hoensbroech, Count Paul. Fourteen Years a Jesuit. New York, 1911.

Von Kubinyi, Victor. Behind the Curtain. Seemore, Chicago, 1913.

    Through Fog to Light. Seemore, South Bend, 1914.

Von Zedtwitz, Baroness. The Double Doctrine of the Church of Rome.
    Revell, New York, 1906.
    A German aristocrat maintains that a gulf between "esoteric"
    Catholicism and "exoteric" Catholicism renders the whole religion
    invalid.

RELIGIOUS CONTROVERSY

Walsh, Lilian A. **My Hand in His**. Henry E. Walter, Ltd., Worthing,
England, 1957.
Clearly expressed reasons for her conversion from Rome to low-church
Anglicanism.

Wonderful Name. Henry E. Walter, Ltd., Worthing, England, 1967.
Sequel to My Hand in His.

Witcutt, W. P. **Return to Reality**. SPCK, London, 1954.
Brief but sincere account of an English idealist who went from
the Church of England to Rome and back again.

C. Ecumenical

Asmussen, H., et. al. **The Unfinished Reformation**. Fides, Notre Dame,
Indiana, 1960.
The Catholic Church must be willing to change.

Berkouwer, G. C. **The Second Vatican Council and the New Catholicism**.
Presbyterian and Reformed, Philadelphia, 1965.
A careful analysis of what did change and what did not change at
Rome a decade ago.

Bianchi, Eugene C. **John XXIII and American Protestants**. Corpus, Washington
D. C., 1968.
Excellent study of how Protestant attitudes toward Rome changed in the
days of Pope John and President Kennedy.

Bosc, J., et. al. **The Catholic-Protestant Dialogue**. Helicon, Baltimore,
1960.
Primarily European orientation.

Brown, Robert McAfee and Gustave Weigel. **An American Dialogue**. Doubleday,
New York, 1960.
A classic of pre-Vatican II ecumenism.

Brown, William Adams. **The Church, Catholic and Protestant**. Scribners,
New York, 1935.
An excellent interpretation of the mystique of Roman Catholicism,
Protestantism, Orthodoxy and Anglo-Catholicism. Author urges that
each religion learn from the others.

Callahan, Daniel, et. al. **Christianity Divided: Protestant and Roman
Catholic Issues**. Sheed and Ward, New York, 1961.
Thoughtful and positive.

Clinchy, Everett Ross. **The Growth of Good Will: A Sketch of Protestant-
Catholic-Jewish Relations**. New York, 1953.
Movements toward interfaith reconciliation portrayed.

Clyde, Walter R. **Interpreting Protestantism to Catholics**. Westminster,

104

Philadelphia, 1959.
Fair and balanced.

Cowan, W. H., ed. Facing Protestant-Roman Catholic Tensions. Association
Press, New York, 1960.
Ideas on how to resolve conflicts in the community.

Cristiani, L. and J. Rilliet. Catholics and Protestants: Separated
Brethren. Newman, Westminster, 1960.
A French Catholic-Protestant encounter.

Gregg, Able J. (Mrs.) New Relationships with Jews and Catholics.
Association Press, New York, 1934.
Pioneering ecumenism.

Hudson, Winthrop S. Understanding Roman Catholicism: A Guide to Papal
Teaching for Protestants. Westminster, Philadelphia, 1959.
Attempts to be objective.

Scharper, Phillip, ed. American Catholics: A Protestant-Jewish View.
Sheed and Ward, New York, 1959.
Stimulating and provocative essays.

Stuber, Stanley. How Protestants Differ from Roman Catholics. Association,
Press, 1961.

A Primer on Roman Catholicism for Protestants. Association Press,
New York, 1953, 1965.
Fair and factual presentation.

Tavard, George H. Protestant Hopes and Catholic Responsibility. Fides,
Notre Dame, Indiana, 1960.
Lucid and realistic.

Waddams, Herbert M. The Struggle for Christian Unity. Walker, New York,
1968. Blandford, London, 1968.
An excellent history of the tendencies toward unity throughout twenty
centuries of Christianity.

Wells, David F. Revolution in Rome. Intervarsity, Downers Grove, Illinois,
1972.
A Neo-Evangelical interpretaion.

D. Pre-Ecumenical

Here is a representative sample of pre-ecumenical critiques of Roman
Catholicism by Protestants. They are noted primarily for their criticism
of official Catholic doctrine on religious liberty and separation of church
and state. One should cross-reference this material with the section on
the history of religious conflict (Chapter IV).

Autry, Allen Hill. Warning Signals, or Romanism and American Peril. Little Rock, Arkansas, 1911.

Barnum, Samuel W. Romanism As It Is. Connecticut Publishing Company, Hartford, 1872.

Barrett, E. Boyd. Rome Stoops to Conquer. Julian Messner, New York, 1935.

Berkouwer, G. C. The Conflict with Rome. Zondervan, Grand Rapids, 1958. The Dutch Reformed scholar critically examines the principal tenets of Catholic dogma.

Boettner, Loraine. Roman Catholicism. Presbyterian and Reformed, Philadelphia, 1962.

Cadoux, C. J. Catholicism and Christianity. George Allen and Unwin, London, 1928.

Calloway, Timothy Walton. Romanism vs. Americanism. Atlanta, 1923.

Carroll, Anna Ella. The Great American Battle or the Contest Between Christianity and Political Romanism. New York, 1856.

Christian, John T. America or Rome, Which? Louisville, Kentucky, 1895.

Colacci, Mario. The Doctrinal Conflict Between Roman Catholic and Protestant Christianity. T. S. Denison and Company, Minneapolis, 1962 A former Roman Catholic priest and professor who is now a Lutheran theologian ably summarizes the pre-Vatican Council differences between the faiths. Includes an excellent bibliography.

Elderkin, George W. The Roman Catholic Problem. Vantage, New York, 1954.

Hammond, William. The Roman Catholic System, Destructive of our Spiritual, Domestic and Social Welfare. Protestant Association of South Africa, Capetown, 1944.

Howell-Smith, A. D. Thou Art Peter; A History of Roman Catholic Doctrine and Practice. Watts and Company, London, 1950.

Jones, Ilion T. A Protestant Speaks his Mind. Westminster, Philadelphia, 1960. A sharply critical look at Roman Catholic political and educational policy. Calls upon Protestants to enter the political arena to resist Catholic aggression and preserve Protestant culture.

Martin, Joseph H. The Influence, Bearing and Effects of Romanism on the Civil and Religious Liberties of our Country. New York, 1844.

McCallen, Robert S. Strangled Liberty, or Rome and Ruin. Columbia Book Concern, St. Louis, 1900.

McKim, Randolph H. Romanism in the Light of History. Putnams, New York, 1914.

Morrison, Henry Clay. Romanism and Ruin. Pentecostal Publishing Company, Louisville, 1914.

Nichols, James Hastings. Primer for Protestants. Association Press, New York, 1950.

Paul, Francis J. Romanism and Evangelical Christianity. Hodder and Stoughton, London, 1940.

Pelikan, Jaroslav. The Riddle of Roman Catholicism. Abingdon, Nashville, 1959.

Pickett, Leander Lycurgus. Uncle Sam or the Pope, Which? Pentecostal, Louisville, 1916.

Poynter, J. M. The Reformation, Catholicism and Freedom. Epworth, London, 1929.

Schaff, David S. Our Father's Faith and Ours: A Comparison Between Protestantism and Romanism. Putnams, New York, 1928.

Strong, Josiah. Our Country. New York, 1886. (Reprint by Belknap Press of Harvard University, 1963).
A paradigm of Nineteenth Century anti-Romanism by a Congregationalist minister who was opposed to immigration, parochial education and Catholic influence on public policy. This book went through many editions, selling 175,000 copies until 1916. The chief librarian of Congress compared its influence with that of Uncle Tom's Cabin.

Subilia, Vittorio. The Problem of Catholicism. Westminster, Philadelphia, 1964.
A Waldensian Protestant view of certain fundamental Catholic beliefs which are irreconciliable with Protestantism.

Tipple, Bertrand M. Alien Rome. Protestant Guards, Washington, D.C., 1924.

Van Dyke, Joseph S. Popery, the Foe of the Church and of the Republic. People's Publishing Company, Philadelphia, 1871.

Von Hase, Karl. Handbook to the Controversy with Rome. 2 volumes. Religious Tract Society, London, 1909.

E. Anti-Ecumenical

Beach, Bert Beverly. Ecumenism: Boon or Bane? Review and Herald, Washington, D. C., 1974.
A Seventh-day Adventist scholar's concern that ecumenism, by placing

primacy on unity above liberty, may lead to the destruction of religious liberty.

Blanshard, Paul. Paul Blanshard on Vatican II. Beacon, Boston, 1966. A balanced and realistic assessment of the Second Vatican Council. Author records the achievements and weighs them against the unfinished business of needed reform. Provocative.

Carson, Herbert M. Roman Catholicism Today. Zondervan, Grand Rapids, 1965. A Baptist pastor from Northern Ireland casts a skeptical eye on the Vatican Council and claims that in no essential doctrine has Rome changed at all. (Also see his shorter work The New Catholicism, London, 1965.)

Henderson, Ian. Power Without Glory: A Study in Ecumenical Politics. Hutchinson, London, 1967. An acerbic look at ecumenism and alleged "Anglican imperialism" by a Scottish theologian who believes that the ecumenical movement has actually divided rather than unified Christendom.

Lowell, C. Stanley. The Ecumenical Mirage. Baker, Grand Rapids, 1967. A phillipic against many of the presuppositions of the ecumenical movement. Author believes that denominational distinctives are being submerged in an ecumenical mishmash, with particularly undesirable consequences for Protestantism.

Murch, James DeForest. The Protestant Revolt. Crestwood Books, Arlington, Virginia, 1967. A fervent denunciation of ecumenism and the policies pursued by the National Council of Churches.

Chapter IX

MISCELLANEOUS PROBLEM AREAS

There are always a few subjects that just don't fit in anywhere and
they are included here. Such minor church-state disputes as church wealth
and tax exemption, religion and the law, interfaith marriages, and Sunday
legislation are considered in this chapter.

A. Church Wealth and Tax Exemption

Balk, Alfred. The Religion Business. John Knox, Richmond, 1968.
     Brief introduction to the subject with some documented material.

Gollin, James. Worldly Goods. Random House, New York, 1971.
     A massive study of Catholic Church financial resources with special
     attention to the U.S.A.

Larson, Martin and C. Stanley Lowell. Praise the Lord for Tax Exemption.
     Robert B. Luce, Washington, D.C., 1969.
     A documented study of all church wealth, much of it tax exempt, in
     the U.S. by two able researchers. Early paperback edition entitled
     Church Wealth and Business Income. A revised edition, entitled
     The Religious Empire will be published by Robert B. Luce in 1976.

Lo Bello, Nino. The Vatican Empire. Trident, New York, 1968.
     A top-notch reporter surveys the incredible riches of the Vatican.

Lo Bello, Nino. Vatican, U.S.A. Trident, New York, 1972.
     A good study of Catholic Church wealth in the U.S.

Manhattan, Avro. The Vatican Billions. Marshall Morgan and Scott,
     London, 1972.
     A prominent critic of the Vatican surveys the whole history of its
     accumulation of wealth and property.

Pallenberg, Corrado. Vatican Finances. Owen, London, 1971.
     A Vaticanologist's reasoned assessment.

B. Religion and the Law

Berman, Harold J. The Interaction of Law and Religion. Abingdon,
     Nashville, 1974.
     Thoughtful essays on the mutually dependent interactions between law
     and religion.

Blechler, James E., ed. Law for Liberty: The Role of Law in the Church
     Today. Helicon, Baltimore, 1967.
     A refreshing look at canon law in an age of change.

Dignan, Patrick J. A History of the Legal Incorporation of Catholic Church
     Property in the United States, 1784-1932. Catholic University Press,
     Washington, D.C., 1935.

An excellent survey of a highly specialized area of church-state relations.

Eppstein, John C. N. The Catholic Tradition of the Law of Nations. Burns and Oates, London, 1935.
A treatise on international law and Catholic principles.

Fellman, David. Religion in American Public Law. Boston, 1965.
The influence of theology on civil law surveyed.

Kurland, Philip. Religion and the Law. Aldine Publishing Company, Chicago, 1962.
A survey of ways in which law reflects or changes religious opinion.

C. Interfaith Marriages

Colacci, Mario. Christian Marriage Today: A Comparison of Roman Catholic and Protestant Views. Augsburg, Minneapolis, 1958 (revised 1965).
Complete elucidation of Roman Catholic and Protestant teaching on marriage, with special reference to mixed marriages.

Hurley, Michael, J., ed. Beyond Tolerance. Geoffrey Chapman, London, 1975.
An important new look at interfaith marriage, with case studies from Britain, Germany, Switzerland, France, Australia and Ireland. Contains papers delivered at the International Consultation on Mixed Marriages held in Dublin in September 1974 and an address by Irish Foreign Minister Garret Fitzgerald on the political and legal implications of mixed marriage problems in Ireland.

Lowell, C. Stanley. Protestant-Catholic Marriage. Broadman, Nashville, 1962.
A thorough survey of the inherent problems involved in such a union because of the Roman Catholic Church's intermarriage stipulations.

Stewart, Oliver. Divorce Vatican Style. Marshall, Morgan and Scott, London, 1971. (U.S. distributor - Attic Press, Greenwood, South Carolina).
A critique of Papal canon law on annulment and divorce, which emphasizes, in the author's view, the inconsistencies of Vatican policy.

West, Morris L. Scandal in the Assembly. New York, 1971.
The great Australian Catholic novelist calls for more charity and flexibility in Vatican marriage and divorce policies.

D. Sunday Legislation

Blakely, William Addison, ed. American State Papers Bearing on Sunday Legislation. National Religious Liberty Association, New York, 1891.

MISCELLANEOUS PROBLEM AREAS

A collection of documents showing the efforts of the sabbatarians
and the Lord's Day Alliance to compel Sunday closing observances.

Johns, Warren L. Dateline Sunday USA. Pacific Press, Mountain View,
1967.
Excellent history of Sunday-closing laws in American law and politics.

Lewis, Abram Herbert. Sunday Legislation: Its History to the Present Time
and its Results. Appleton, New York, 1902.

HOW TO STAY INFORMED

Keeping up with developments in the church-state field is not easy. Neither is keeping in touch with new books in the genre, especially when there are 40,000 new books in all subjects published in the U.S. each year and 35,000 new titles in the United Kingdom. I would suggest the following three publications for all students of this area:

Church & State (8120 Fenton Street, Silver Spring, Maryland, 20910. Subscription $5.00 a year, monthly except August) is a specialized journal of news and analysis which reports all the significant church-state news from around the world. The magazine also reviews about 50-75 books a year.

Journal of Church and State (Box 380, Baylor University, Waco Texas, 76703) is a scholarly journal published three times yearly. It contains a number of good book reviews in each issue, plus in-depth articles on many subjects.

Liberty (6840 Eastern Avenue N.W., Washington, D. C., 20012) is a beautifully designed and well edited bi-monthly published by the Religious Liberty Association of America and the Seventh-day Adventist Church. It is informative and written in a popular vein.

In addition, several other periodicals often include excellent church-state articles. They are:

America (106 West 56th Street, New York, 10019) the "official" weekly publication of U.S. and Canadian Jesuits. It is often informative and lively.

Christian Century (407 South Dearborn Street, Chicago, Illinois, 60605) is still the semi-official journal of liberal Protestantism. It has lost much of its prestige and lustre, but is beginning to make a comeback.

Christianity Today (1014 Washington Building, Washington, D. C., 20008) is an evangelical fortnightly which reports occasional church-state news.

Commonweal (232 Madison Avenue, New York, 10016) is the best Catholic journal in the U.S. by every criteria.

The Tablet (48 Great Peter Street, London SW1P 2HB England.) is an international Catholic weekly that is unexcelled in the quality of its reporting, analysis and coverage of new books.

Suggestions for Book Collectors:

Most of the books in this bibliography are, regrettably, out of print and must be located in antiquarian bookshops. I have been most fortunate in locating six bookshops specializing in religion:

Christian Classics - 205 Willis Street, Westminister, Maryland 21157.
Emerald Isle Books - 539 Antrim Road, Belfast, Northern Ireland BT15 3B
Nelson's Book Room - Lydbury North, Shropshire SY7 8AS England.
Noah's Ark Book Attic - Stony Point, Route 2, Greenwood, South Carolina 29646.

HOW TO STAY INFORMED

Pax House - P.O. Box 47, 29 Lower Brook Street, Ipswich, Suffolk
    IP4 1AH England.
Richard Booth Ltd. - Hay-on-Wye, Hereford HR35 DQ England.

INDEX OF AUTHORS

AUTHOR INDEX